I HAVE AUTISM

—————•—————

WHO WILL BE MY VOICE?

A Mother's Search for Answers

By
Mary Ann Puckett
map77@cox.net
405-919-0051

Cover Design: Ashley C. Thomas
Sweet Fig Photography

ISBN (Print) 978-0-97679-551-3 (Ebook) 978-0-97679-552-0

DEDICATION

This book is dedicated to the memory of Elizabeth Grace Filby, BA (Hons) Cert.Ed. FRSA., who was a friend, helper, and valued resource to my son Stephen and me.

January 30, 1952–June 26, 2016.

ACKNOWLEDGMENTS

There are a number of professionals I want to recognize for their valuable contributions in sharing information that has improved the quality of life for my son, Stephen, who has Early Infantile Autism and Lennox-Gastaut Syndrome.

Dr. Russell Blaylock, M.D., is a retired neurosurgeon, published author, and has worked as an assistant professor of neurology. On several occasions Dr. Blaylock provided information to me on natural supplements that greatly reduced Stephen's seizure activity, which I believe has been lifesaving.

Dr. Stephanie Seneff, PhD., is a Senior Research Scientist at MIT, and has also provided me with information that has proven beneficial for my son, such as ways to activate sulfur in his body to help with his medical diagnosis of encephalopathy. She has additionally made suggestions on important dietary changes for Stephen. In 2013, she was a contributing author to a published paper, "Is Encephalopathy a Mechanism to Renew Sulfate in Autism?"

Grace Filby, BA (Hons), Cert.Ed. FRSA, was a Science and Engineering Ambassador, in Reigate, England. Grace was an advocate for getting critical information out about the use of bacteriophages to stop deadly infections like MRSA and E.coli. Stephen was treated with a bacteriophage in 1990, which I believe saved his life. In 2007 Grace was awarded a Churchill Traveling Fellowship through the Winston Churchill Memorial Trust. The Fellowship afforded her the opportunity to travel to international bacteriophage conferences where she met leading scientists and doctors. In 2008 Winston Churchill's daughter, Lady Soames, presented Grace with the Churchill Fellows, *Silver Medallion* award for her research on phage therapy. Phages are natural waterborne viruses that attack and destroy bacteria. In 2015 Grace was invited to Buckingham Palace where she received recognition from Her Majesty Queen Elizabeth for her research on bacteriophages. Grace was a very dedicated, caring person, and I felt honored to call her my friend. Sadly, due to her passing in June 2016, she will be greatly missed. Her vast knowledge of health information will be missed by health professionals, and I will personally miss her ongoing support of my advocacy for autism. We also shared the connection of knowing from experience what phage treatment can do for critically ill people.

I also want to acknowledge Dr. VJ Conrad, M.D., and Dr. Heather K. Geis, M.D. Dr. Conrad began treating Stephen when he was totally nonverbal at the age of six. I will always credit her for Stephen being verbal today because of her decision to do early intervention with allergy testing and to check his amino acid levels, which were addressed with supplements recommended by the laboratory that evaluated his bloodwork. She was also the only doctor who was willing to prescribe a sleep medication for Stephen to help our family recover from the eight years of sleep deprivation due to Stephen's daily meltdowns. Dr. Conrad is a doctor who listens and thoughtfully makes every attempt to find answers for her patients.

Dr. Geis has been Stephen's psychiatrist for the past twenty-one years. She is a very compassionate doctor, who has literally provided a shoulder for me to cry on. Her willingness to help me find information on autism is without measure. As she stated in her endorsement, she has been with us through times of great joy and of overwhelming adversity, and for this I will forever be truly grateful.

Many thanks to these wonderful and caring individuals who have helped me learn so much on this autism journey.

Contents

INTRODUCTION

As I look into the eyes of my thirty-five-year-old autistic son Stephen, I can't help but wonder what thoughts are going through his mind. Does he understand that I miss him when he's not with me, and will he ever understand how deeply I love him? Parents of children like my son spend countless hours pondering thoughts like these. Thoughts about who will say I love you to Stephen and, more importantly, what will happen when I can no longer care for my child? The uncertainties of this life are a given, but when you have a child that is disabled, the intensity of this uncertainty is endless. If only Stephen's autism was just a bad dream, then I could suddenly wake up and find that he is like other young men who are driving, dating, holding down a job, getting married, having children, and living independently. Unfortunately, in Stephen's case, he will never be able to do those things, and his autistic condition is not just a bad dream, it's a reality.

CHAPTER 1

Diagnosis and Hurdles

On June 10th, 1996, at age fourteen, Stephen was diagnosed by Dr. Bernard Rimland, PhD., with Early Infantile Autism, also known as Kanner's Syndrome. Dr. Rimland was a research psychologist who wrote, lectured, and researched information about autism for many years. The diagnosis that Dr. Rimland gave Stephen means that my son functions on the lower end of the autism spectrum. My husband and I had been trying for many years to get doctors to give a definitive answer as to what was going on with Stephen because real concerns for his future existed. As an adult, Stephen's level of functioning is still very limited. His cognitive level is at about five to six years of age. He can do some academic tasks like solving simple addition and subtraction problems using a calculator, and reads with a very limited level of comprehension.

Even though Stephen made little eye contact from very early in his life and appeared to be content being alone in his own world, I still attempted daily to make a meaningful connection with him. Using various methods, in an attempt to get into Stephen's world, we discovered very early that he reacted positively to music, as many children with autism do. I played various types of music for him, ranging from classical to popular and country western. When he was around one year old, I additionally started playing a series of records for him from a phonics program called Play'n Talk, developed many years ago by a woman in California named Dr. Marie LeDoux, PhD. The catchy tunes on the Play'n Talk records seemed to hold his attention, even though he was still not making eye contact. When the music started playing, Stephen stopped whatever he was doing and listened very intently.

At age six, Stephen finally began to talk, and it quickly became evident that he had the ability to sound out and read simple words from newspapers and magazines. I cannot state definitively that the phonics program helped Stephen develop this skill, but I personally believe it did play a part. During this same timeframe, one of the teaching assistants in Stephen's classroom reported that they were shocked when he suddenly picked up a book on display and read thirty pages out loud. She said he then just put the book down and walked away as if nothing was unusual about what he had just done. Even today his spelling is still quite good, but his reading comprehension remains very limited.

School services Stephen began receiving in his special education class were occupational therapy, physical therapy, and speech therapy; these continued through high school. Yet, even after receiving those therapies for many years he is still unable to do what would be simple everyday tasks for most people. Stephen cannot tie his shoes, shave, comb his hair, and bathe without assistance. His limited dexterity and motor coordination assures that he will definitely be dependent on others for the rest of his life.

A secondary diagnosis for Stephen is a severe seizure disorder called Lennox-Gastaut Syndrome. LGS is unbelievably difficult to manage and a very cruel progressive form of epilepsy. People who suffer from LGS experience many various kinds of seizures. My husband and I, my mother, my mother-in-law, and my neighbor all observed Stephen suffer seizures within days of his diphtheria, pertussis (whooping cough), and tetanus (DPT) vaccine. However, his pediatrician dismissed my report of the seizures and told me not to worry. In chapter 5 I will go into more detail about LGS.

In Stephen's first year of life we noticed that he was not meeting normal developmental markers, so I began asking the pediatrician and other doctors about the possibility of Stephen being autistic. The doctors responded to my questions with evasive answers, such as, "Well, he does have some autistic tendencies," and "Give him time; he will do things when he is ready." Those doctors really missed the mark because Kanner's Syndrome is not simply autistic tendencies, it is full blown autism.

In fact, Stephen exhibited all seventeen of the autism behavior characteristics, published many years ago by the Autism Society of America. Behaviors such as avoiding eye contact, playing with toys inappropriately, throwing crying tantrums, resisting being cuddled, and resisting changes in routine, are some of the characteristics on that list. From early in his life Stephen's daily and nightly tantrums were a major issue. The meltdowns began in his first few months of life, and the problem progressively became so unbearable that I would literally beg doctors for help, but none of them offered anything that helped us.

One doctor suggested that we simply put Stephen in his room for time out. We tried that a couple of times, but it only caused him to become more upset, and more aggressive. Another reason that time out did not work with Stephen was because he was incapable of comprehending cause and effect. Obviously those doctors had little knowledge about autism and no comprehension of the challenges with which parents of a child with autism are attempting to cope. Not to mention how miserable the autistic child is when he is having the meltdowns. When Stephen finally began to speak, at the age of six, his conversation was repetitive in nature (echolalia), and that trait hasn't changed to this day. Even now he begins the day by talking about vacuum cleaners, Judge Judy, and George Strait. His constant repetition of these topics is labeled as perseveration, which in many cases can be indicative of a brain disorder.

Stephen can list the names of almost every vacuum on the market and what type of bag is required for each one. He also loves to tell people that Hoover vacuum cleaners are made in North Canton, Ohio. Like the character in the movie *Rain Man*, Stephen has to watch all court programs that are on television every day. He will ask me over and over, "What happened to the plaintiff?" or, "What happened to the defendant?" *Judge Judy* is his favorite television show, and he loves to repeat her comments, such as, "Do I have stupid written across my forehead?"

Stephen has watched the video of George Strait's, *Live at the Astrodome* more times than I can begin to count. He knows the names of every musician in George Strait's band, as well as the instrument each member plays, and of course, the name of George's band, which he loves to share with everyone he meets. Stephen has attended two George Strait concerts, and both times it was fun just watching Stephen's incredible excitement about being there. During the concerts he laughed, clapped his hands, and repeatedly screamed, "Yay! George Strait." Stephen's big concern at both concerts was what color of hat George would be wearing: black or white. At the last concert, George was wearing a black hat which bothered Stephen because he was anticipating that George would wear a white hat. Some lengthy conversation was required to explain to Stephen that the color of George's hat was okay. Stephen tells me every day that he wants to shake George Strait's hand. If that ever happened, I sure hope George has on the correct color of hat, or Stephen will surely bring it up to him. Stephen's dream may seem small to most people, but it means the world to him.

Even though Stephen fixates on various things to talk about, his receptive and expressive language is quite limited. These limitations make it difficult at times for him to understand what is being said to him and restricts the breadth of information he is able to communicate. Many autistic children interpret what is said to them literally. For example, if a teacher says something in class such as, "Okay, students, put your eyes on the board," an autistic child may have difficulty understanding and react in a manner that is unacceptable. It is important for schools to offer one-on-one assistance for children like Stephen because an assistant for the autistic student can explain what the teacher means and possibly avoid upsetting the student.

Stephen's limited expressive language makes it difficult for him to tell me if he feels pain or if he is sick and he may not say much about it. It's only when something is seriously wrong he might say, "I'm sick," or "It hurts to death." In 2012 Stephen had a serious health issue that took us months to figure out. The problem began showing up at mealtime when he would sometimes only take one bite of food and wanted nothing else to eat. This was unusual for Stephen because normally he loves to eat and almost always asked for second helpings. As a result of this extreme change in his eating habits, he lost seventy-seven pounds over a period of seven months. He began eating less and less every day and then started throwing up after only taking a few bites. This happened often enough that we began keeping a large pan nearby when Stephen was attempting to eat. I was reporting this change to his doctors when it first began, and we made numerous trips to the emergency room in an attempt to find out what was going on. Sadly, during the hospital emergency room visits, the doctor didn't investigate, just simply reported that Stephen was dehydrated because he was vomiting so much. The doctor ordered an IV to hydrate Stephen then sent us on our way with a prescription for nausea medication.

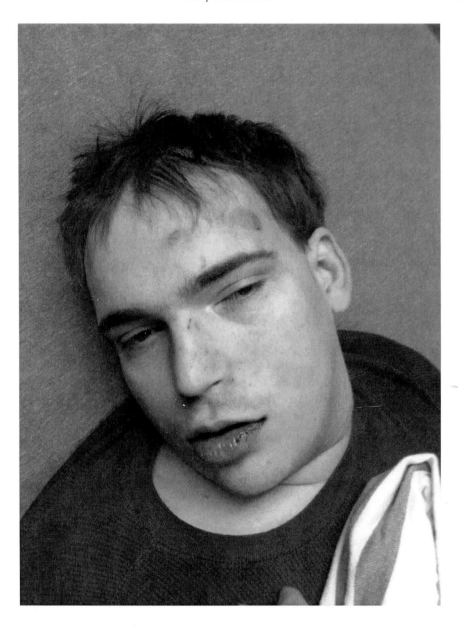

After several months of going in and out of the revolving door of the emergency room Stephen became so ill that he started having frequent grand mal seizures. Eventually, a grand mal seizure caused him to fall and land face down in our hallway. The fall was so hard it broke Stephen's jaw, knocked a bottom tooth completely out, and misaligned several of his bottom teeth. We called an ambulance, which rushed him to the hospital where he had emergency oral surgery. Ironically it was April 1, April Fools' Day, and not even close to being an April fool's joke.

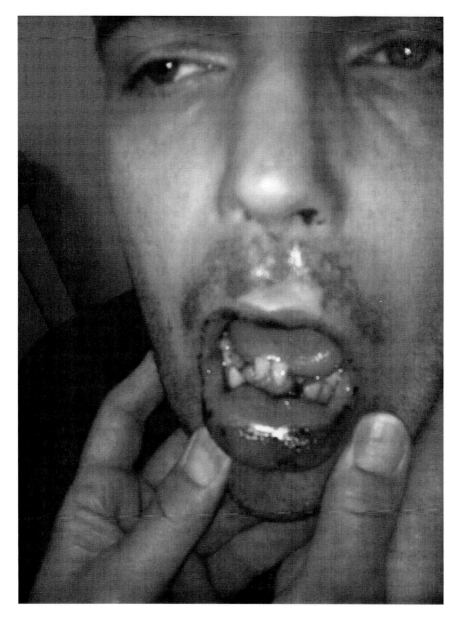

After the oral surgery I spoke with Stephen's primary doctor's office about the weight loss, increased seizure activity, and how sick Stephen apparently was. Finally, a nurse practitioner said they were going to refer Stephen to be evaluated by a gastroenterologist, which I feel should have been done long before he became so ill and had the terrible fall.

When we saw the internist, he decided that a gastrointestinal endoscopy for Stephen should be scheduled. He said the procedure would be done at the hospital with sedation. Afterwards the doctor came to the waiting room and said to my husband and me, "No wonder he is so sick, he has five large ulcers." He said the ulcers were probably the reason why Stephen did not want to eat and couldn't keep food down. Bless Stephen's heart. How painful that must have been for him to suffer all those months, but as I pointed out, his limited expressive language made it impossible for him to tell us that it hurt when he was trying to eat.

Situations like this are why people like Stephen are at risk and always need an advocate to be their voice. Caregivers must always be proactive to seek medical help for people like my son when something serious is suspected. This is one of my many major concerns I have for Stephen's future.

You can't always rely on one doctor's opinion, so sometimes obtaining a second opinion is necessary when a problem persists. Unfortunately, in Stephen's case I had been telling doctors for months that something was seriously wrong with him, but no one listened. A friend, whose uncle was a doctor, explained to me why she thought Stephen did not receive better investigative treatment in the emergency room for the persistent vomiting and weight loss. She said her uncle told her that people like my son are sometimes referred to as GOMERS, an acronym for, "Get out of my ER." I was horrified at hearing this.

After my friend shared that information with me, I have often asked nurses and doctors we encounter if they have ever heard the word "GOMER" used in reference to people like Stephen. Many have said they were sad to report that they have heard doctors refer to patients like Stephen in that way. After thirty-five years of navigating the autism journey, I have met many parents who share similar stories of their challenges in trying to get help for their children in a doctor's office or in an emergency room. Parents not only have difficulty getting help from doctors and hospitals for their children, but also getting help from school systems, therapists, dentists, and other professionals. Why do families like ours have to continue to fight an uphill battle to get what is needed for our loved ones?

In the following chapters I will discuss what I believe parents and advocates for autistic individuals need in order to win some of these battles.

CHAPTER 2

Regrets

When I held my newborn son for the first time thirty-five years ago, I looked at his perfectly formed body and had no idea of the suffering and obstacles he would endure in his future. Had I known then, what I know now about vaccine injury, autism, and seizures, I could have made better decisions that I believe with all my heart would have made a huge difference in Stephen's quality of life. Prior to Stephen's birth in 1981, the only knowledge I had in regards to autism was a small bit of information on a video I had watched in a college course on early childhood development.

Stephen's autism issues began to manifest when he was just an infant and rapidly increased over time. His behaviors really took us by surprise, and we were completely lost as to what was really going on with him. I had no clue that early intervention programs even existed. At the time, information regarding autism awareness was just beginning to emerge, and I knew of no resources from which I could get help for Stephen during his early years of development.

I am assuming that the reason for such limited resources on autism in the early 1980s was the smaller population of children on the spectrum, perhaps due to fewer children being properly diagnosed. Furthermore, I personally believe fewer children had autism at that time. Until the release of the movie *Rain Man*, in 1988, most people had never heard of the disorder.Stephen was around seven years old before I finally met another mom who had a child, like my son, with autism on the severe end of the spectrum. She was the first person who helped me learn about existing therapies and suggested resources we could access for Stephen. Early intervention therapies such as sensory integration (SI) could have been very useful in helping Stephen overcome his eating and chewing difficulties. SI therapists are trained to address issues dealing with the five senses, which can be problematic for many children with autism. For example, many children on the spectrum are very picky eaters because of the different food textures, which can upset them due to sensory issues. A lot of children with autism do not like being touched because touch can also be over-stimulating and upsetting for them. Certain sounds, smells, and visual input can be over-stimulating. Temple Grandin is a noted adult with autism who explains in her books and lectures how such things are a problem for people with autism because, like her, all five senses are turned up to volume ten, and people with autism cannot modulate down the intensity of incoming stimulants.

Applied behavioral analysis (ABA) is another therapy that has been proven to be quite effective in helping to remediate many of the behavior issues that autistic children and adults may exhibit. ABA can aid people with autism in making exceptional progress. ABA works by using techniques such as verbal prompts or cues with positive reinforcements, modeling (visual demonstration), and task analysis where lists of tasks are written out in very specific detail. Prior to Stephen being in a wheelchair and attending a sheltered workshop, I had a large picture communication chart posted on one of our walls that I went over every morning with Stephen before he left. We discussed the pictures, which helped Stephen understand the order and events of his day. Behavior problems and inappropriate social skills were something Stephen needed help with from very early in his life.

As Stephen grew older, I learned about another therapy called *social stories* by Carol Gray. Social stories have proven to be very effective because they teach the art of communication through providing examples. This therapy works exceptionally well for higher functioning children who are diagnosed with a form of autism on the higher end of the spectrum called Asperger Syndrome. I had the great privilege of meeting Carol Gray several years ago at a National Autism Conference. During our brief conversation I thanked her for all her hard work and what she has done to effectively help so many who suffer with social issues.

Not knowing about early intervention therapies for Stephen is one of my regrets. The biggest regret of all is that I did not have early knowledge about vaccines and their contaminants. Thimerosal, for example, is a mercury based preservative which is added to a number of vaccines, and is a deadly toxin. Pharmaceutical companies add thimerosal to vaccines because it preserves the shelf life by keeping down the growth of bacteria. One article I read stated that it also removes the need to refrigerate some vaccines. So, adding mercury to vaccines is economically beneficial for pharmaceutical companies because the vaccines can be stored for longer periods of time. However, mercury happens to be one of the most deadly toxins on the planet, and pharmaceutical companies are aware of that. For instance, if one drop of mercury should be discovered in front of my house, officials would report hazardous materials and evacuate the neighborhood. This scenario recently played out in a neighborhood not far from where we live as a locally reported breaking news story. The story was that a few drops of a hazardous material, mercury, had been discovered in a neighborhood. Emergency responders wearing white hooded suits were instantly called in to be on the scene to clean up the spill, and news stations were additionally on site to cover this serious event. Yet, to this day I cannot comprehend how the pharmaceutical industry can justify putting a deadly toxin, such as mercury, into the arm of a baby or an adult. Thimerosal is still in some flu vaccines that people are being given, not to mention other vaccines on the market that contain toxins.

My mother was with me the day I took Stephen for his first Diphtheria, Pertussis, Tetanus, (DPT) vaccination at two months of age. His reaction to the vaccine was immediate and so severe that my mother mentioned she was worried about it. She said that she had never seen a baby react to a vaccine the way Stephen did. From the moment he received the vaccine, he started screaming and hung his vaccinated arm limp to his side. His crying was high pitched, a piercing scream, and he was inconsolable. By the time we got home from the doctor Stephen was running a high temperature of

104 degrees. We gave him Tylenol as I had been advised by his doctor, but it didn't bring his temperature down.

His crying continued for at least twenty-four hours, literally non-stop. My mother and our next door neighbor tried to help me. We passed him back and forth and walked the floors with him, trying to soothe him. Within a few days of Stephen receiving the DPT shot he began to have multiple full body tremors about forty times a day. At that time I was not aware of *infantile spasms.* Even though I was a new mom, I knew this was not normal because I had never held a baby that shook the way Stephen did.

My mother and mother-in-law started witnessing Stephen's daily tremors, and they both told me to be sure and tell his pediatrician what was happening because they realized that something was wrong. When I told the pediatrician about Stephen's daily tremors, he told me not to worry. He said that I was simply being "an over-reactive mother," and dismissed my concerns. Years later I learned that what I was calling "tremors" were infantile spasms. Infantile spasms can be associated with a condition called "West Syndrome", and are treated with hospitalization and administering steroids to bring down inflammation in the brain. However, if the spasms go untreated they can sometimes later lead to a condition called "Lennox-Gastaut Syndrome" (LGS), and as I reported earlier, Stephen is now diagnosed with LGS. From what I have read on this subject, if the infantile spasms had been addressed by the pediatrician, Stephen may not have developed LGS. But remember, as the doctor said I was being, "an over-reactive mother." That pediatrician has been deceased for many years; however, if he was still living I can assure you that I would let him know what he has put Stephen and our family through for the last thirty-five years.

Over the years, several doctors have actually agreed with me that the spasms Stephen experienced after the vaccine were probably caused due to swelling in his brain. That brings us to the next big question: what was in the vaccine that caused the swelling? Maybe in the early 1980's steroids were not used as a standard treatment for infantile spasms, but if the treatment was available, I wish that Stephen had received some help with what was happening to him. The daily spasms were frightening to watch as well as concerning for me, not to mention how miserable they must have been for Stephen. The cause of Stephen's infantile spasms, and now his diagnosis of LGS, sure seem like a missing piece of the autism puzzle to this over-reactive mother.

Lennox-Gastaut Syndrome is considered the worst form of epilepsy because it is progressive, and in many cases it is fatal. Statistics state that about two percent to five percent of people with epilepsy fall into the category of LGS. According to reports from the National Institutes of Health, about thirty percent of children on the autism spectrum can develop some type of epilepsy, but not necessarily LGS. Unless a person has had hands-on experience in dealing with epilepsy, most are only aware of, or have witnessed, grand mal seizures. In my quest to learn more about seizures, and what is available to help people like my son, I was amazed to find that there are literally hundreds and hundreds of different types of seizures that can occur with epilepsy.

A few include the following:

1. Rolandic seizures occur mostly during sleep. I know from experience about Rolandic seizures because I was diagnosed with them at the age of eight and was put on Dilantin. Mine were grand mal seizures, and I would have them only in the mornings as I was awakening. The seizures continued until I was about sixteen.

2. Gelastic seizures are referred to as laughing or crying seizures. They are usually brought on by a sudden burst of energy. The word "Gelos" in Greek means laughing.

3. Masticatory seizures are referred to as eating seizures and can involve chewing, smacking, tasting, and lip licking. When Stephen has this type of seizure, we have sometimes performed

the Heimlich maneuver to save his life because he can choke on the food he is eating.

The list of different kinds of seizures that people can develop is quite lengthy. In chapter 5 I will discuss more about LGS and the multiple types of seizures that Stephen has and does experience.

CHAPTER 3

Autism versus Marriage and Family

Autism changes everything in life. All hopes, dreams, and aspirations are altered forever. Most couples begin life together making plans for their future, and setting goals to achieve their dreams. Our marriage started out that way, but when the unexpected happens, such as having a child diagnosed with autism, everything in our life was altered dramatically. After Stephen's birth, and once autism symptoms began to emerge following vaccinations, our personal goals switched course. We began to think only in terms of how to care for Stephen and how to improve his quality of life. Any ambitions and goals we once had for our married life and future were then permanently set on a different course.

From very early in my life, I was quite involved with music and had been singing and performing from the age of four. As an adult I played guitar, playing and singing for audiences in clubs and on television and radio. I was also a published songwriter. For many years I had devoted countless hours to voice lessons and piano and guitar lessons and practice. My husband and I met in a music store when I stopped in to ask if they had a guitar teacher who was taking new students. My husband, Tom, is a classical guitarist and also played professionally.

I knew music would always play a major role in my life. However, after autism made its debut, my personal goals changed from playing, singing, and songwriting to just trying to get enough sleep to make it through the day. Daily caregiving for a child with autism consumes your entire life. As a result, I had very little time or energy left at the end of each day for other activities such as sitting down to enjoy playing or listening to music, reading the newspaper, or even watching a television program. Stephen's severe meltdowns that emerged early on kept us awake all day, and every single night. My husband and I took shifts for the first eight years of

Stephen's life. Not only does autism consume your physical strength, but it also affects your mental stamina, which makes it difficult to think clearly.

When Stephen was two and a half years old our daughter Laurel was born. So then we had a newborn as well as addressing Stephen's issues. I know there are thousands of parents who have similar circumstances, and a high percentage of the caregivers are single moms or dads.

Stephen's nightly tantrums were hard for our daughter because of the relentless and sleepless nights. As an adult she has been diagnosed with posttraumatic stress disorder (PTSD). When Stephen would awaken, he would start screaming at the top of his lungs, and Laurel would be startled awake and also begin to cry. I truthfully don't know how we survived those early years. It was only by the grace of God. Stephen's unusual sleep patterns and violent outbursts were so demanding that we had countless sleepless nights, which left my husband, daughter, and I extremely sleep deprived. The lack of rest created a great deal of tension in Tom and my marriage. Having an occasional unsettled sleepless night is one thing, but when it becomes a consistent pattern of waking up night after night, year after year, at all hours, to a screaming toddler, then a screaming teenager, and finally a screaming adult, life becomes increasingly unbearable.

I still believe that Stephen's infantile spasms were contributing to him waking up every single night in such a frantic state. He screamed, threw things, and attempted to scratch or bite me if I were within close range. We had to literally hold him down on the floor, as gently as possible, to keep him from injuring himself or one of us. Stephen's meltdowns had started at night, but soon began occurring during the day as well. In the early years, each time I discussed the sleeping problems with doctors, they would tell me to just leave Stephen in his crib for a 'time out'. They said the meltdowns would eventually stop, and he would go to sleep. The doctors were wrong.

Once Stephen began to crawl, and eventually walk, he could then move about the house throwing objects and breaking anything he could get hold of. The few times I tried following the doctor's advice of putting him in time out were complete disasters. Placing Stephen in his baby bed, per the doctor's advice, didn't work because he quickly learned to climb over the side of the bed and would end up on the floor screaming and kicking the bedroom door until he bruised his feet. Sometimes he would pick up objects or toys in his room and use them to beat the door, leaving indentations in the wood. His nightly tantrums were so intense that his screaming equaled the volume of a freight train roaring past our house, which was another reason why simply putting him in his room was not the solution. As he grew older, the violence increased. He often broke windows out of the house, knocked holes in walls, and went after anyone in reach. This violence and destruction went on every day, year after year, and all we could do was try to console him and keep him from hurting himself or others. Laurel spent most of the time in her room alone, listening to the chaos on the other side of her locked door.

Family time, family vacations, or any outings into the community also became very challenging because of Stephen's meltdowns. Most of the time, we would have to alter our plans and stay home. There were times when Stephen acted out at church, and people would just shake their heads or make comments, saying things like, "You're just going to have to put him somewhere." "Where do you suggest I put him?" I would respond. No answer back to my question was ever offered. I was not trying to be contentious about this comment; I was simply trying to make the person reconsider what they had said to me and gain some sort of understanding. Other families could get in their cars and drive away from the situation, something we didn't have the luxury of doing. This was our life.

Realistically, who was going to take Stephen and deal with his extreme behaviors? And, would the person who made the comment at church be willing to just take their own child and put him or her somewhere? Of course they wouldn't.It doesn't take very long before the day-to-day pressures of autism begin to mount to the point that the topic of divorce is discussed. In many cases, the father suggests divorce as a solution. I have heard one statistic that ninety percent of the marriages with one or more autistic children end in divorce. Many of the mothers I have met at autism conferences or meetings on autism are divorced, and they would tell me that their husbands actually left right after their child was diagnosed.

One mother, who reached out to me a few years ago, explained that she was happily married and working as a dental assistant before her son was born and diagnosed with autism. She said shortly after her son was diagnosed, her husband filed for divorce. She told me that now she is on welfare and food stamps, and is staying up all night with an out-of-control child. When these wonderful mothers share their tragic stories with me, I can't help but believe that God will bless them for their dedication to their children.

In our case, my husband did not leave, but quite honestly divorce has been the topic of discussion many times due to constant mental stress, physical overexertion, and financial strain. As earlier mentioned, autism not only affects marriage, but also siblings. Autism is a family disability. Stephen's younger sister, Laurel, is now thirty-three years old, but has suffered extreme pressures throughout her life due to her brother's serious issues.

Many times when my husband and I were required to focus our full attention on Stephen during a crisis, Laurel was left waiting in the background. Every single day, Laurel witnessed her brother's extreme behaviors and fighting, which troubled her very deeply, and she was many times the target of his aggression. As a child, she started having sleeping issues and trouble concentrating. My father once asked, "Why doesn't Laurel ever smile?" In addition to Stephen's behaviors and violence, she also witnessed his seizures and was aware of the strain Stephen's actions and illness was putting on the whole family.

When Stephen would be unconscious (postictal) after a seizure, it was always upsetting for Laurel. While waiting for emergency help to arrive, she would frequently ask if her brother was going to die because of his appearance during the postictal period. When Stephen was postictal following a seizure, there were times when my husband had to perform CPR until the ambulance arrived.

As a child, Laurel never experienced one day when her father would arrive home from work and say, "Let's put the kids in the car and take them to a movie," or "Let's take a drive around the lake and stop at the duck pond and feed the ducks." These are only two examples of the many things that families like ours never were able to do. Stephen simply could not cope with additional outside stimulus because it was too overwhelming for him, which always resulted in him having a meltdown. Anytime we attempted to go anywhere as a family, we would return home with everyone in tears. There were very few happy childhood memories for Laurel. She lived every day in a survival mode. It almost became common place to have police cars and ambulances arriving during the day and in the middle of the night to help us with Stephen. As a result of our lifestyle, Laurel now suffers with and has a medical diagnosis of panic attacks and extreme anxiety. Laurel's diagnosis requires her to be on medications in order to cope, and make it through each day. In this past year she was additionally diagnosed with schizophrenia.

The world needs to understand that autism is a disability that impacts the entire family and carries with it a lot of psychological pain. I have personally felt a sense of guilt at times because it's as though I sacrificed one child for another, but what were my options? This question is rhetorical because I love both of my children equally; no options existed for me.

The financial strain placed on our family was another major issue. Doctor visits, medications, ambulance runs, and hospital stays are very costly, and are still an issue at Stephen's present age because Medicare does not cover all that is needed for him. For example, he had a tooth broken off at the gum line while he was incarcerated in jail. The cost of getting implants to repair the damage was very expensive. When we took him to an oral surgeon about the broken front tooth, fixing one tooth turned into the removal of four teeth because the tooth next to the broken one had become infected, and the other two teeth on each side of the damaged teeth were loose. In our state, after a disabled person turns twenty-one, dental coverage is not available through Medicaid.

Now that I am retired, Stephen's primary insurer is Medicare, and his secondary insurer is Medicaid. I buy a dental plan to pay for cleanings and fillings, but I still pay for anything over that out of pocket. Medicare covers the cost of pulling teeth but not of replacing them, so after Stephen had his teeth damaged in jail, I did not want him to go the rest of his life without front teeth. We took out a large loan for implants. That loan took several years to repay.

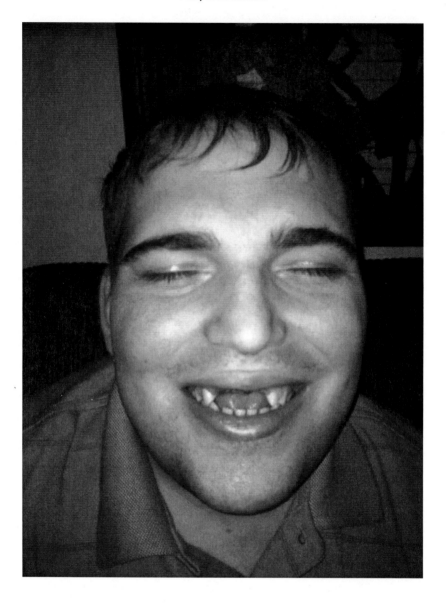

We have many times had to sell items from our home to cover the cost of Stephen's doctor visits and medications. There were times I would tell the pharmacy to fill only half of a prescription, and we sold something to pay for the other half of the medication. My husband once sold his car and rode a bike to work for six months so that we could pay medical bills.

These are some examples of what parents of medically needy children go through in order to provide care for their children.

CHAPTER 4

Holding on to Hope

In light of all of the family dynamics that autism affects, parents and caregivers must learn to adapt and face the challenges of autism, as well as they can. We can't give up on our children and must continue to hope for better awareness and help for them from schools, the medical community, and from new therapies to help them develop to their highest potential. I have never given up on searching for ways to improve Stephen's quality of life, and many times the search has paid off. Stephen's autism has put me in contact with many caring compassionate people, which has often led me to new interventions to try with him.

Thousands of families like ours learn to manage and deal with autism issues one day at a time. At local and national conferences I have purchased booth space for my previous book, "Take Him Home and Love Him/A Story of Autism and How to Cope with It." I chose that title because when Stephen was a baby, doctors would tell us repeatedly to just take him home and love him. Over the years I have heard other mothers tell how they were also told to do that with their autistic children. As I stated in the first book, I don't know of any mother to whom it would be necessary to say that, because in most cases mother's instinctively love their children.

When I attend conferences, it is not unusual for mothers to approach my booth with tears running down their faces. They begin telling me their personal autism stories because they so desperately need someone to listen and understand the difficulties they face each day. Having faced many of the same challenges, I am always more than happy to listen to these stories. Having someone hear them out is cathartic for them, and my heart goes out to them because I completely understand their plight.

The idea of autism was introduced to the world on a large scale by the movie *Rain Man*. I believe we are still on the tip of the iceberg as far as raising public awareness about the extreme stress this disability brings with it, and an understanding of the different dynamics of each level of the spectrum. The movie *Rain Man* depicts an individual who is much higher functioning than Stephen. Those very high functioning people, who are at the top of the spectrum, are labeled "savants." Statistically, only about two percent of the autism population falls into the savant category.

A high percentage of people on the spectrum are diagnosed with Asperger Syndrome. Most of those children can many times function in regular classes at above, or on grade level with modifications. I know a number of moms who have Asperger children. Some of their children learn to drive, go to college, and are able to live independently as adults, yet they still have social deficits, and other issues that can be very challenging.

Throughout the broad autism spectrum disorder (ASD) many individuals have what is referred to as, splinter skills. This means that certain areas of their brains can function at such an incredibly high level that it amazes people who witness this gift. For example, from a very young age Stephen has exhibited the ability to sound out and spell lengthy, multi-syllabic words that many average people might have difficulty pronouncing.

In comparison, splinter skills for the individuals in the savant category are so beyond belief that scientists and doctors are still trying to comprehend the mind-boggling ability of these individuals who execute unheard-of tasks, as depicted in *Rain Man*. It's hard to understand how these extremely high functioning savants can perform at such a high level, yet simple daily life skills such as counting from one to ten or tying their own shoes is impossible in many cases.

An example of someone who functions in this way is Derek Paravicini, who is a young autistic savant who lives in London and has a remarkable story. Derek is blind from birth and also has a severe learning disability, yet he is a composer and a musical genius, with perfect pitch. He is often referred to as, "the human iPod." Derek plays the piano entirely by ear and can play a wide variety of music, from classical to popular music, with great accuracy after hearing a song only once. He has performed in Europe and the United States and has been featured in television documentaries such as *60 Minutes*. There are a large number of YouTube videos about this wonderful young man.

Kim Peek was also a savant who was considered to be the inspiration of the character Raymond from the movie *Rain Man*. He was born in Salt Lake City, Utah, and was referred to as a *megasavamt*. Unfortunately, after many years of being cared for by his loving father, Kim passed away in 2009 at the age of fifty-eight from an apparent heart attack, followed by his father's passing in 2014. Kim was born without the bundle of nerves that connects the two hemispheres of the brain, which resulted in his neurons making unusual connections. Due to the absence of Kim's bridge or bundle of nerves called the corpus callosum, which is what connects the two cerebral hemispheres of the left and right side of the brain, he had an expanded memory capacity. Even with his expanded memory capacity it's reported that on psychological tests Kim scored below 87 on IQ tests.

Kim required help from his father with daily living skills such as shaving and dressing and other things that require fine motor skills. In spite of such limitations, Kim had the ability to read both pages of a book at the same time, using his left eye for the left page, and his right eye for the right page, and was able to recall everything he read with about ninety percent accuracy. His father said that Kim would read a book then place it upside down to indicate that he had read it. Kim was tested on his recall ability at many schools and public venues. He would take questions from the audience on a vast array of topics and astounded everyone with his accuracy in recalling the answers with such exactness. Kim's father stated in an interview that his son required thirty hours a day and ten days a week care. What a loving, dedicated dad Kim had.

Stephen Wiltshire is another brilliant savant who lives in London, and is referred to as "The Human Camera." He has the unique ability to see and remember everything in precise detail. His unparalleled ability is recorded in several videos. In some of the videos, Stephen is being flown in a helicopter over different cities, such as Rome, where he quietly looks out the window of the helicopter and observes every street, building, window, bridge, sign, light pole, and other features of a complicated cityscape.

After they land, Stephen is taken into a room with large panels of paper and charcoal pieces, and he uses these to replicate what he saw during the flight. After he completes the drawings, a transparent photo of what Stephen observed is placed on top of his drawing to check for accuracy. Amazingly, Stephen's recall of what he observed during the flight is almost completely correct.

Many people are aware of Dr. Temple Grandin, PhD., who I briefly mentioned in chapter 2. She is a professor of animal science at Colorado State University and is highly recognized for her many lectures and books written about her life as an autistic person. Among her numerous accomplishments, Dr. Grandin is known for her humane design of circular cattle chutes used by slaughter houses for cattle. She explains that she came up with the idea of the circular design after living for a few years on a cattle ranch with her aunt. She said she observed how the cattle would pause briefly at every ninety degree turn as they were going through the chutes to the slaughter house. She said she could identify with their sense of fear because, like her, they were afraid of what they would encounter once they turned the corner. It's reported that her circular designs of cattle chutes are widely used because they do not cause a fear reaction in the cattle, thus avoiding an adrenalin release. The result is a better quality of meat. I have read that about two-thirds of the meat packaged in the world is provided through her circular designs.

In 2010 Dr. Grandin received a Peabody award for an HBO TV movie based on her life, which starred Emmy Award winning actress Claire Danes as Temple Grandin. I have had the privilege on several occasions to speak with Dr. Grandin about Stephen, and she gave me some excellent ideas of things I could try with him. I told her about his obsession with vacuum cleaners. Her suggestion was to get the book *How Things Work*, for him. It has a section on vacuum cleaners. She said he might grow up to invent a new type of vacuum. Dr. Grandin is such a fascinating person, and I have high regard for her willingness to continuously advocate toward raising awareness about autism by sharing her personal stories.

Only a small percentage of people on the spectrum are savants. A higher percentage of people on the spectrum are diagnosed with Asperger Syndrome. These individuals can also accomplish great things, but still have their limitations with social skills or behaviors. A close friend of mine has a son diagnosed with Asperger Syndrome, and he graduated from college with a 3.8 grade point average. She told me he made A's in the most difficult math classes offered at the university he attended, yet he still needs guidance on decision-making and saying things appropriately to others. She said she will sometimes have to correct him on something he said to someone, and then she explains to him what he should have said.

As for lower functioning people like Stephen, his diagnosis of Early Infantile Autism, made by Dr. Bernard Rimland, places him on the lower end of the autism spectrum. Dr. Rimland researched and wrote a book in 1964, entitled *Infantile Autism*, following the diagnosis of his son Mark. Dr. Leo Kanner, who was an autism pioneer, wrote the forward for the book. Dr. Rimland continued to do research on autism and was one of the early founders of The Autism Society of America, along with Dr. Ruth Sullivan, PhD., who also has a son with autism.

In 1967 Dr. Rimland additionally founded the Autism Research Institute (ARI) in San Diego, California, which promotes alternative treatments for autism. He was a big proponent of using B6 as a supplement for children with autism.

Stephen was a teenager in 1996 when we finally had a real diagnosis for our son, thanks to Dr. Rimland. We had waited many years for an actual written diagnosis to help us better understand what to expect for his future development. We are so grateful to Dr. Rimland for his help in giving us this long-awaited diagnosis. With his passing in 2006, the world lost a brilliant advocate for people with ASD.

Stephen has made a lot of progress in certain areas over the last thirty-five years, yet he still requires constant one-on-one care. Added to his diagnosis of low-functioning autism, is his second diagnosis of Lennox-Gastaut Syndrome, which I will discuss in the next chapter. In spite of his many challenges, Stephen has his good days. However, his father and I continue to hold onto hope that new therapies and medications will continue to be developed to help our son.

CHAPTER 5

Lennox-Gastaut Syndrome

Like most people, I had never heard of Lennox-Gastaut Syndrome until Stephen received the diagnosis when he was a teenager. Apparently LGS is rare enough that medical doctors and nurses will often ask me to explain what it is, how to spell it, or may ask how it affects Stephen. Some doctors say they have heard of it, but don't fully understand what it entails. LGS is a very difficult form of epilepsy and is challenging to treat because it presents with multiple kinds of seizures. Most children with LGS also have an associated developmental or intellectual disability. Only two percent to five percent of people with epilepsy are diagnosed with LGS. It usually has an onset before age eight and peaks between the ages of three to five years.

LGS shows clear parallels to West Syndrome (infantile spasms), which I discussed in chapter 1. When Stephen began having the multiple daily tremors, right after receiving his first DPT vaccine, I reported it to his pediatrician. The doctor listened as I explained what I was calling tremors, which were happening at least forty to fifty times per day, but he simply dismissed it. In my heart I knew there was something seriously wrong with my son.

At a local teaching hospital I was recently invited to speak to a group of second year resident doctors about autism. During the presentation I made a specific request to the future doctors. I asked them to please listen carefully when a parent comes to them with concerns about their child and try to help that parent find answers because their concerns are real, and what they're reporting may be life-threatening to the child. I ended the talk with a well-known quote, "Be kind to the people you meet, they are fighting a hard battle." I have always believed that this particular quote has special application for any parent who is caring for a child that is disabled.

Stephen's Early Infantile Spasms or West Syndrome was a signifi-cant turning point for him. A medical description of West Syndrome (WS) describes the spasms he exhibited as lightning attacks, and if those spasms go untreated WS can develop into LGS. Now with LGS, Stephen can present with many types of seizures daily. One type is tonic-clonic, also known as grand mal seizures. Stephen is very confused after this type of seizure and will sometimes be incontinent and lose consciousness for hours. Another type is atonic, or no tone seizures. This means that various muscles in his body suddenly go limp. If atonic seizures occur while Stephen is in a seated position he will topple over to one side. If he is standing when they occur, he usually ends up on the floor. Stephen once had an atonic seizure, also known as drop seizures, while he was transferring to the sofa. His loss of muscle tone in his legs caused him to fall and break his left foot. His assistant was holding onto Stephen's arm at the time, but was unable to do little more than slightly break the fall.

Two years ago Stephen had a drop seizure when my husband was trying to transfer him from his wheelchair into the bathroom. Stephen went straight down, landing with his weight of 240 pounds on his right leg. I was in the living room when it happened, and I heard a very loud pop that sounded like a gunshot. My husband screamed for me to call an ambulance because Stephen had broken his leg. While we were waiting for the ambulance to arrive, Stephen's eyes were filled with tears and his bottom lip was pressed out. He kept repeating, "I have a boo boo, how fix it?" I told him the doctors would have to fix it and reassured him that we would be at the hospital with him. The fall not only broke both bones in his leg, but also partially split the tibia vertically. The break required surgery to place a titanium rod in his leg, and several screws to piece the bones together.

The myoclonic seizures that Stephen has can occur more often if he is tired. This type of seizure causes his muscles to quickly spasm, and he thrusts his arms or legs out from his body, remaining very stiff for a brief moment. During a myoclonic seizure, I have witnessed Stephen's muscles contract so tightly that he can suddenly go from a seated to a standing position with no warning. The first time I saw this happen he was fourteen and in the hospital undergoing telemetry. On the first day of telemetry, the neurologist began to slowly withdraw his seizure medications in order to increase seizure activity. During telemetry they were videotaping Stephen twenty-four hours a day, seven days a week, and he also had electrodes connected to his head for an electroencephalogram (EEG), which continuously records brain waves. The doctor asked me to stay in the room with Stephen so I could push a button each time I observed a seizure, or "event", as they referred to it. He explained that by pushing the button, the video tape would be marked so that the doctors could later come and observe the events of the day. When Stephen had the myoclonic seizure I referred to, it was so sudden and surprising that I jumped and yelled out, "What was that?" Over an intercom, a person in another room, who was monitoring the seizure activity said, "That was a myoclonic seizure." I told him that was the first time I had ever witnessed that type of seizure.

From very early in his life Stephen has also had many masticatory seizures, which are eating seizures. They only occur when he is chewing. Masticatory seizures cause him to suddenly thrust his head backward, which can make him choke on his food and sometimes aspirate the food or drink into his lungs. Stephen has had aspiration pneumonia three times due to this type of seizure.

Absence seizures are also referred to as petit mal seizures. They last only a few seconds, and Stephen will just stare off into space. Unless a person has had experience in recognizing absence seizures, most would not realize anything is happening. During the petit mal seizures he simply has a brief impairment of consciousness. If he is talking when the seizure occurs, it will often cause him to forget what he was trying to say. Stephen's complex partial seizures (grand mal seizures), can result in his consciousness being impaired for long periods of time, and sometimes for several hours. Doctors refer to this unconscious state as a postictal period. The longest postictal period I have witnessed with Stephen has lasted ten hours. The "ictal" period is the seizure itself, and the "post" period is when the brain is recovering from the trauma of the seizure. A neurologist explained to me why the postictal period happens. She said that after a seizure the brain is very tired from firing of so much electrical energy and needs to rest. She said the brain has to shut down the conscious state to allow it to conserve enough energy to keep the autonomic nervous system working. The autonomic nervous system is what acts unconsciously to regulate the function of heart rate, digestion, respiration, urination, and other major bodily functions.

I am sad to report that even though Stephen's serious seizure disorder can be life threatening for him, he has been turned away from hospitals numerous times during seizure activity. Over the years we have made many trips by ambulance to hospitals when Stephen was unconscious after a seizure. We were advised to do this by his neurologist. The doctor said she preferred that we err on the side of caution when he is postictal because the hospital is equipped to constantly monitor his blood pressure. She explained that when he is postictal his blood pressure could suddenly drop to a dangerously low level, and the machines would be able to pick that up. However, if we kept him at home during the postictal period, we would not be aware if something like that happened. Additionally, the hospital would be able to do blood tests to see if any medication changes were needed.

Many times after arriving at the hospital, with Stephen having seizures and aggressively attacking people, the emergency room doctors would immediately tell us that they could not admit Stephen for a medication adjustment because they were just not equipped to deal with his aggressive behaviors related to his autism. They would however do blood tests to check his levels, give him something to briefly calm down, and tell us to follow up with his neurologist. They would then release him back to us. The problem with the hospital offering such limited help for Stephen has always been that his seizures and aggression are something my husband and I are less equipped to handle than the emergency room staff. Usually, by the time the emergency room completed the paperwork for dismissal, the calming medication they had given Stephen when we arrived would have worn off. So then driving home, with Stephen fighting us in the van, was always a nightmare. There were times when Stephen would grab my husband from the back seat while Tom was driving, which caused Tom to swerve into oncoming traffic. When this happened, it was always amazing that we actually made it back home without wrecking the van and killing one of us or some innocent person. When I explain this problem to emergency room doctors, they just listen to me, with a blank look on their faces, and then proceed to release Stephen anyway.

Stephen's medical records thoroughly document that he can become aggressive while he is having seizures. However, the emergency room doctors seem to pay little attention to his documented history, and basically let us know that we were just out of luck with no place to turn. All we have ever requested was that a hospital offer us some help by holding Stephen long enough to get him stabilized. The Americans with Disabilities Act states that a hospital cannot refuse treatment based on a person's diagnosis, and we have never asked a hospital to treat Stephen's autism, just help us with the seizures and aggression, which can be corrected with medication changes.

Historically, when emergency room doctors have turned Stephen away because of his autism, I would ask them where they suggest I take him for the seizures. One doctor responded by patting my arm and telling me that he didn't know, but to just remember that we could always come back. I could not believe he actually said that and was thinking, "Come back for what?" Was that doctor aware that one of the chief complaints in medicine today is the rising cost of patients who repeatedly go to the emergency rooms, not to mention the cost of calling ambulances time and time again because we could not get Stephen's seizures and aggression under control? There were weeks when we made as many as three trips to hospitals by ambulance trying to get help for Stephen. The trips to the hospital were sometimes recommended by police and emergency responders who were repeatedly coming to our home to help us with Stephen. The fact that the hospitals would then release Stephen back to our custody, as fast as possible, makes it obvious that there is definitely a disconnect somewhere in the medical system. We have been caught too many times in a revolving hospital door with Stephen. However, hospitals will admit people violent due to a myriad of other reasons, but not Stephen because he has autism. I would hate to be those doctors who will someday have to answer to God for their disregard of Stephen's suffering and the dangerous situations we have endured. What kind of world do we live in today that allows this kind of discrimination toward a person because he is disabled?

In January of 2010, we took Stephen by ambulance to a local hospital for seizures and aggression. The hospital quickly brought in a case manager who recommended that Stephen go to a psychiatric hospital, ninety miles away, for a medication adjustment. The woman told us that the hospital where we were was not equipped to help us. She said it was our only option. So here we were again, up against an impossible medical system.

During Stephen's stay in the psychiatric facility, where he had been many times, the doctor in charge put Stephen on a medication called FazaClo, which is an atypical antipsychotic medication that is mainly used for schizophrenia. FazaClo, also known as clozapine, is sold under the brand name Clozaril. Clozapine reportedly has some serious side effects that can be potentially fatal. When the psychiatric hospital called two weeks later for me to come and pick Stephen up, I immediately noticed that he was having difficulty walking and his movements were very jerky. Stephen's assistant was with me that day, as well as my friend Beth, who has an autistic son. After putting Stephen into the van and driving about two blocks from the hospital, Stephen said he wanted to talk to his dad. I called my husband and handed the phone to Stephen's assistant, who was seated next to him. He handed the phone to Stephen to say hello to his father. Suddenly my cell phone was flying to the front of my van and hit the windshield. I stopped the van and looked back to see what was going on. Immediately I recognized that Stephen was having repeated myoclonic seizures, and his muscles were in spasms, which was causing him to thrust his arms and legs out from his body. Stephen also began getting very loud and aggressive. My first thought was to call Stephen's psychiatrist to ask her what we should do at that moment because we had a ninety-mile trip ahead of us. Stephen's doctor got on the phone and her first question was, "What medication changes did they make at the psychiatric hospital?" I told her the doctor had prescribed a new medication for Stephen I had never heard of called FazaClo. Stephen's doctor responded by telling me that he could not take that medication, so we are going to have to take him off of it. However, she said it was not a drug that can just suddenly be stopped, and we would need to slowly titrate it down.

As it turned out, the FazaClo information sheet inserted in the drug package states, in big bold print, if a person has a seizure disorder, do not to take the medication under any circumstances. This is a perfect example of how Stephen gets shuffled around, and his life is put at risk because he has autism. It took about one month to get Stephen off of that potentially deadly medication. His last dose of FazaClo was on a Saturday, and Stephen's assistant was at the house to take him to the mall to look at vacuum cleaners, which is one of Stephen's favorite things to do. After they left for the mall, I had plans to attend a wedding shower. I always keep my cell phone on, and within reach, because I stay in a constant state of anticipating calls about Stephen. Sure enough, right after arriving at the shower my phone rang. It was Stephen's assistant calling to explain that Stephen had a seizure while looking at vacuums. He said he grabbed Stephen's arm and tried to break the fall as Stephen was going down. After the seizure, Stephen was not able to stand or walk.

This made me wonder if Stephen had possibly had a stroke because he left for the mall in a run to the assistant's car earlier in the day. The assistant told me an ambulance was on the way and wanted to know where they should take Stephen. I told him to have them take him to a hospital that was only about two miles from the mall, and I would meet them there. When I arrived at the hospital they had padded the sides of the bed because Stephen was having one seizure after another. He was also incontinent, and nurses were coming in to change the pads under him each time he lost control of his bladder. When the emergency room doctor finally came in, he acted irritated. He asked me why we brought Stephen to their hospital because he has a competent neurologist at another hospital. I told the doctor that when I receive a call that my son has had a seizure and cannot walk, the first thing that comes to mind is that he possibly had a stroke. Then I reminded him that people are always advised to go to the nearest hospital if they suspect a stroke. Then the doctor asked me, "Well, why can't he walk?" I said, "Doctor, I don't know why he can't walk, that's why we are here."

I could tell the doctor was acting upset that Stephen was in his hospital. He finally said they would do an x-ray to see what it might tell them. After the bloodwork and x-ray results came back, the doctor came in to say that they didn't see anything wrong but would put him in a soft brace for his leg. Meanwhile, Stephen was still in the bed having seizures, urinating on himself, semi-conscious, and complaining that he was hurting. My husband was also at the hospital, and we were both sitting in the room with Stephen waiting to see what the hospital was going to do for him. After being there for several hours, we never saw the doctor again, only a nurse who walked in pushing a wheelchair. As she handed me a stack of papers, I asked what the papers were. She said they were release papers. I said, "Are you serious, look at him, he is barely conscious, can't walk, and he is having seizures." The nurse only responded with, "Sorry, doctor's orders," and she walked out. Needless to say, Tom and I were speechless.

I asked Tom how we were supposed to get a semi-conscious person into a wheelchair, and then get him home. I stepped into the hallway and was calling for someone to come and help us, but no one was in sight. It was if the emergency room was totally abandoned, and no one was answering the call button on the bed. Finally, my husband said he would back up to the bed, then he wanted me to push Stephen forward and lift his arms so he could grasp Stephen's hands and pull them around his neck. While holding Stephen's hands tightly around his neck, he lifted Stephen from the hospital bed and turned slowly to lower him into the wheelchair. This was all so unreal, and I could not believe it was actually happening. I always understood that a hospital is supposed to help someone safely leave the facility, and until a patient steps foot into the car to leave, safety is the hospital's responsibility. We eventually managed to get Stephen into the wheelchair and exit the emergency room. Then I stood outside, holding Stephen in the wheelchair, while my husband brought the van from the parking lot to pick us up. When we arrived home and got Stephen into the house, I told Tom I was going to call an ambulance because Stephen was still having seizures and needed help. When the paramedics arrived, they took one look at Stephen and said, "This guy needs to be in a hospital." I told them that we had just come from a hospital that refused to help him.

They loaded Stephen into the ambulance and took him to another hospital. When we arrived at the second hospital, the doctor came right in, and he called for a neurologist. However, because it was a weekend, it took the neurologist several hours to get to Stephen. When the neurologist finally came in, he immediately asked, "How long has he been having these seizures?" I told him what had happened many hours earlier at the mall. A CAT scan of Stephen's head was ordered to rule out a stroke, and they took more x-rays of his leg.

After looking at test results, they concluded that Stephen had apparently pulled some muscles as he fell during the seizure, so they ordered a larger splint for his leg. Additionally, the neurologist increased one of his seizure medications and told us to follow up with his doctor. After this ordeal was over, I obtained copies of the medical records from both hospitals Stephen had been in that day. You could not have found two reports that contrasted more. The first emergency room doctor wrote in his notes that upon dismissal the patient was alert, back to baseline, and ambulatory; none of which was true. The doctor's notes from the second hospital, only one hour later stated, upon arriving at the hospital, the patient was disoriented to time and place, was incontinent, and was having seizures. I know that doctors take an oath to do no harm, but I seriously doubt if that first doctor believed what he said when he took that oath.

Two months after the previous hospital fiasco, in April of 2010, Stephen was taken by ambulance three different times, over a three-day period, to a local hospital for seizures and aggression. Before each trip to the hospital, our local police were called to the house to help us with Stephen. Once the officers got him calmed down a bit and handcuffed, they would call an ambulance. Upon arrival, the doctor gave us the same song and dance of how Stephen needed to be admitted until the seizures were stabilized, but because he has autism they were just not equipped to handle the situation. On the third visit, April 5, 2010, Stephen kicked a security guard because he was so out of control. As a result, he was arrested, handcuffed, and taken to the county jail where he was charged with a felony assault. You can view the local NBC news story about this on YouTube: Autistic Man Arrested.

The officer who filed the charge told me that it was obvious the hospital was not going to help Stephen and said that by filing the assault charge it would allow him to get the treatment he needed in the medical section of the jail. The officer said that hopefully the next morning a judge would write and order to force a hospital to take Stephen in and treat his seizures. Sadly, that was not what happened.

Not realizing what the outcome would be, our only option at the hospital was to agree with what the officer was telling us. We knew that Stephen needed medical intervention from somewhere because he was completely out of control. My husband and I could not consider putting Stephen in a car and driving back home with him kicking, biting, head butting, and trying to choke us. It was a highly dangerous situation, and Stephen needed medical attention, if the jail would provide that.

When the police officer from the jail came to escort Stephen, he began talking to him as if he was able to comprehend what was being said to him, like most twenty-eight-year-olds. He said, "Mr. Puckett in just a moment I will read you your Miranda rights, and then I will handcuff you and escort you to the county jail where you will be charged with a felony assault."

I was absolutely beside myself at this point; I have never cried so much in my life. I was watching my son being treated like a criminal. He was just sitting there, drooling, and tipping over with seizures. When the officer finished explaining what was about to happen he asked, "Do you understand what I just told you?" Stephen looked up and said, "But officer, I'm a good boy." Stephen had calmed down a bit at this point because, at my request, the nurse had asked for an order from the emergency room doctor to give Stephen a shot to calm him down before going to jail. I knew that Stephen was going to be scared to death, and my heart was breaking over it.

The officer didn't acknowledge what Stephen said about being a good boy, he just proceeded to handcuff him and took him away to the county jail where he was charged with a felony assault and was held in custody for nine days, with an $8,000 bond. Unfortunately, a judge did not come forward the next day to sign an order to force a hospital to admit Stephen and help him. Additionally, according to the jail records, Stephen did not receive medical treatment in jail, and it was noted that he refused to take his medication I had provided them. After several days in jail, a judge wrote an order that Stephen be taken to the Crisis Center for a psychological evaluation.

I was calling daily to check on Stephen, and they were reporting to me that he was withdrawn in his room or asleep. Finally, I hired an attorney to help us get in to see him. The attorney called the Crisis Center and told them that my husband and I are Stephen's legal guardians, and we wanted to see him. They told us we could come that evening for a brief visit. This was after eight days of incarceration. The attorney was with us at the Crisis Center that evening when they brought Stephen in to see us. A guard walked in holding onto Stephen because he was unable to stand alone. He was staggering, drooling, and still having seizure activity. He was also missing a front tooth, broken off at the gum line, and both of his wrists were bloody and scabbed over from handcuffs, which left scars that took many months to fade.

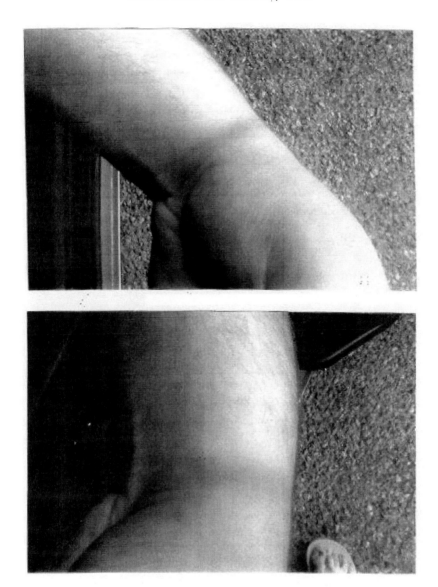

Stephen's appearance and condition at the Crisis Center that night was so shocking. When I asked the guard what happened to his front tooth she said she didn't know. Then I asked the guard if she would bring in the doctor that was on duty because I wanted her to observe Stephen's seizures. When the doctor came in she quickly agreed that he was having seizures and said she would call an ambulance and have him transported to the hospital. However, the doctor recommended the same hospital that had sent Stephen to jail. When I explained to her that he could not go there because that hospital was the reason he went to jail in the first place. The doctor then suggested we try another hospital and I said, "If they will help him that will be fine."

An ambulance was called, and we followed behind it to the hospital. At the hospital we got the same run around as in the past. Stephen was again denied treatment for his seizures because he has autism. The attorney was still with us at the hospital and heard the doctor tell me that neurology would not come and see Stephen for his seizures because they were just not equipped to deal with his autism. I asked the doctor if she was aware that autism is now the number one childhood disability. She commented that she knew they were seeing a lot more people with it. The doctor then said, "I know you're a good mom, let me give you a big hug." It was so unreal to hear the same thing repeated again from another hospital. Stephen was then loaded up and taken back to the Crisis Center even though he was still having seizures.

The next morning, on the ninth day of being in custody, a judge held a hearing and wrote an order that Stephen be released from custody and taken by ambulance to a small hospital ninety miles from where we live to receive treatment in a psychiatric ward. The judge then apologized to my husband and me and said he was so sorry for the way Stephen had suffered. We could not oppose the ruling of the judge, but Stephen's problems were neurological not psychological, so we had to follow his order. Again, no one was listening to us explain why Stephen was having behavior outbursts.

After being transported to the psychiatric hospital I was told they would only hold Stephen for about two weeks and would adjust his medications while he was there. On the day he was scheduled for release from the hospital, I received a call from a nurse in the psychiatric ward. She told me not to come and pick Stephen up because he had a seizure and was unconscious. I asked the nurse if they had monitors to check his blood pressure levels while he was postictal. She told me that monitors were not available in a psychiatric ward, but they were having a nurse go in every twenty minutes to check his blood pressure. The nurse who called said they had witnessed everything I previously tried to explain to the hospital in Oklahoma City before Stephen was taken to jail, and she was very sorry that no one understood what we were dealing with.

Stephen was postictal for several hours after that seizure. The psychiatric ward then held him for several more days. After he was released from the hospital psychiatric ward, another order from the judge at the Crisis Center stipulated we follow up with Stephen's neurologist, who was on staff at the same hospital in Oklahoma City that had refused to admit Stephen on April 5th.

On the day of the appointment with his neurologist, I was anxiously awaiting her arrival. As she entered the exam room she started repeatedly saying how sorry she was about what had happened to Stephen. After her apologies, I made it clear to her that Stephen needed help that week in April, and jail was not the answer. She said she totally agreed with me, but they just don't have staff that is trained to deal with autism. My answer to her excuse was, "If that's the problem, they need to hire people and train them because autism is not going away." Additionally, I pointed out that their hospital will treat and admit people who are on drugs, schizophrenics, alcoholics, gang members, but ironically not someone with autism. I emphasized several times that Stephen had suffered greatly because of what they had done to him.

Once Stephen was finally home, I obtained copies of the records from the county jail and the Crisis Center. The jail records stated that the patient refused medication, and the records from the Crisis Center stated that the patient arrived crawling on his hands and knees, was incontinent, and was mumbling and drooling. Their description of him made me cry even more. Why didn't someone treat him with dignity and at least provide a wheelchair at the Crisis Center to take him into the facility? Instead, they let him crawl in like an injured animal.

If an animal had been mistreated the way Stephen was, the news media would be all over it. There have been many instances where I have watched national news coverage of a dog stranded on a roof, or a kitten trapped in a drain pipe, which I agree needs attention, but there was no national media coverage about Stephen's story? As I previously stated, one local NBC news affiliate covered Stephen's incarceration for the entire week, and gave daily updates on his status. I sent copies of the video news coverage about Stephen's arrest to every single news station across the country, and heard absolutely nothing back from any of them. Even today, Stephen suffers night terrors from the jail stay, and will sometimes awaken in the middle of the night screaming, "Let me up", while he is wildly swinging his arms as if he is fighting. We will never know the truth of what actually happened to our son during his time in custody.

Medical reports state that children with LGS frequently have behavior disorders. Yet, many medical doctors still disagree with us that there is a correlation between Stephen's seizure activity and his behavior, even though it has been recorded in his medical history for years. My husband and I have tried every avenue we hear about attempting to find help for Stephen's seizures. The problem is the limited options of medications for LGS, and not a great deal of information on things besides medication that we can try. LGS is an exceedingly challenging disorder to manage.

In May of 2012, we drove from our home in Oklahoma City, to Cedars Sinai Hospital in West Hollywood for eleven days of evaluation for Stephen in the telemetry unit of the hospital. The appointment at Cedars Sinai had taken many months to schedule, and we were supposed to be in California for the appointment within days of Stephen's diagnosis of the five ulcers that I described in Chapter 1. This made the driving trip more difficult because Stephen was still unable to keep food down, and didn't really want anything to eat. Before we left on the California trip, one of Stephen's doctors wrote a prescription for something to help him sleep through most of the long trip.

Driving straight through from Oklahoma to California with Stephen was a difficult drive, but we actually made it to the hospital twenty minutes before his scheduled check in time. Immediately upon arrival, he was admitted to the hospital and taken to his room. I was so impressed with the hospitals quick action and coordination of the process. Once Stephen was in his hospital gown and bed, one of the first things they did was assign a GI doctor to come in and suggest additional treatment for Stephen's ulcers. Our reason for making the twenty-three-hour drive to the hospital in California was to investigate the possibility of a surgery that might help with Stephen's seizures. The surgery being considered was a corpus callosotomy (CC), which is a serious brain surgery that had previously been recommended for Stephen when he was fifteen years old. The CC is usually performed in two stages, several months apart. It involves cutting the connective tissue between the two lobes of the brain so the seizures cannot fire across the brain from one side to the other. It does not always stop all seizures, but it can sometimes reduce the severity of seizures, primarily the drop attacks that are so dangerous.

Within a couple of hours, a woman named Jody came in and began attaching electrodes at various places on Stephen's head. As with previous telemetry, the electrodes were linked to the equipment that would be recording Stephen's brain waves. This procedure is called an electroencephalogram (EEG), and Stephen was familiar with it. Next, the machines and video cameras were turned on to begin recording Stephen's brain waves and every move constantly. Several doctors came into the room that evening to explain what they would be looking for. They said some of Stephen's seizure medications would not be given at the next scheduled time, and the medications would continue to be slowly discontinued over a period of days. The doctors explained, what we had been told several years prior, that medication reduction would induce seizure activity, or "events." As the medication levels were reduced that evening, Stephen's seizures, or events began to show up pretty fast, as well as his behaviors.

Every evening a doctor, or doctors, would come in to discuss what they were observing on the video recordings. It was a very difficult number of days as the medications continued to be reduced and behaviors were escalating. One evening Stephen became so angry, he got out of bed and was literally picking up one end of the heavy hospital bed and ramming it against the wall. It took several nurses to come in and help my husband and I get him back into the bed. After about eight days of telemetry, the doctors began slowly adding Stephen's seizure medications back into his daily regimen, in order to bring his therapeutic levels back up.

On the last day of telemetry, the team of doctors reported that the slow spike waves of his EEG are characteristic of LGS, however, in Stephen's case, they concluded that he would not be a candidate for the surgical procedure to help control his seizures. They made it clear that if the surgery was performed it would leave Stephen in worse shape than he was at that time. After listening to the doctor's decision, I felt a sense of relief on one hand because he would not be having brain surgery, and at the same time I felt disappointed because it meant the drop seizures would continue. I appreciated the doctor's efforts to evaluate Stephen, but it's unfortunate that a wider range of things weren't available to try in order to help him. Before he was discharged, the doctors recommended that Stephen rest for several days, because the multiple seizures that were induced during telemetry had been very hard on Stephen. After his release we made the long twenty-three-hour drive back to Oklahoma City, which was exhausting for all of us, but was especially stressful for Stephen.

While we were at Cedar-Sinai Hospital, one of the doctors complimented my husband and me by saying that we had apparently taken very good care of our son. He said his oldest patient with LGS had only lived to twenty-four years of age, and Stephen was twenty-eight at that time. The greatest danger that remains for Stephen is his risk of having a fall from a drop seizure that could be fatal. Another risk is having seizures while he is sleeping and suffocating. Doctors have talked to me about the potential dangers of LGS for many years, which is the reason why we stay in such close proximity of Stephen night and day in order to monitor his safety.

Even today there are times when my husband and I will get up in the middle of the night to check his respiration. It's like having a newborn baby, but I guess he will always be our baby no matter how old he is. Still I remain hopeful that more research on LGS will one day find answers for people like Stephen.

CHAPTER 6

Recent Vaccine Information

A tremendous amount of reported information is available today on what is contributing to the increase of autism spectrum disorders (ASD). Testimonials from parents, and articles on ASD, point to the cause being toxins in vaccines and environmental factors. I believe that more investigation of the information reported on vaccine injury and environmental factors is critical. Thousands of parents are coming forward to state that after vaccinations, their children had a severe reaction and were dramatically changed.

For many decades, pharmaceuticals have been adding a mercury-based preservative to vaccines called thimerosal. It's reported that their reason for adding this toxin is to keep down the possible growth of bacteria. Mercury is one of the most deadly elements on the planet, and because of this, I question how a pharmaceutical company can justify putting mercury into a baby's, or an adult's arm, even if they claim that it is only contains trace amounts. I believe that using a toxic compound as a profit point is unethical.

Another source of mercury, (methyl-mercury), comes from eating fish, and most doctors warn their patients about the possible danger of consuming certain kinds of fish while they are pregnant. Yet, flu shots which contain mercury-based thimerosal, (ethyl-mercury), are given to pregnant woman.

Several years ago I had a medical doctor call me to report that she had recently attended a medical conference where she saw actual studies that determined that mercury in vaccines goes into the body and does permanent damage to a child's nervous system. The doctor then said that people will never see those studies, but she wanted me to be aware that they do exist. She said that during the presentation on thimerosal, all she could think of was Stephen. In recent years more and more information is coming forth to substantiate what that doctor shared with me nearly fifteen years ago.

It's interesting that a larger numbers of brave medical doctors are now coming forward to publicly state the danger of vaccines, not only because of the mercury in them, but also other toxic adjuvants. An adjuvant is a substance added to a drug to increase its effect. Dr. Suzanne Humphries, M.D., is a not only a medical doctor, but also an internist and Board Certified Nephrologist who lectures and writes articles and books on the history and dangers of vaccines. She defines herself as a doctor who has learned to think outside the box. Many YouTube videos with Dr. Humphries discussing the dangerous side effects of vaccines are very informative. In one of Dr. Humphries articles, "A Few Things I Know," she states the following, "Vaccines did not save humanity and never will." She also says that, "Vaccines are dangerous and should never be injected into anyone for any reason." She challenges health care practitioners to, "look into the topic of vaccines with an open mind, on their own."

Dr. Humphries states that medical authorities should not have the final word on how doctors treat individual patients in the privacy of their own offices. In her closing statement of this article she asks parents and health care professionals to do their homework because the minds and bodies of future generations depend upon it. I personally completely agree with Dr. Humphries, and I'm thankful she is such an outspoken courageous doctor.

In a YouTube video, Dr. Richard Moskowitz, M.D., talks about the side effects that all medications are known to have. He says that pharmaceuticals seem to get a pass on denying any harm. In reference to vaccines, he addresses the thousands of lawsuits from DPT vaccine injury in the 1980's that resulted in large cash awards. Dr. Moskowitz also details in his videos how natural immunity and vaccine immunity differ substantially. He explains that our immune systems are designed to respond to an infection in a natural way by catching diseases like measles, mumps, and chicken pox, which allows the body to respond acutely to the disease. He says that once the disease has run its course, the result is a strengthened immune system.

I have always personally questioned that if medical authorities claim there is no evidence of vaccine danger, then how have some people recovered money through the courts for their vaccine damaged children? In 1982 Barbara Loe Fisher along with Jeff Schwartz and Kathi Williams, founded The National Vaccine Information Center (NVIC), which is an anti-vaccination advocacy group. In a posted article on their site dated November 2, 2015, "Vaccine Injury Compensation: Government's Broken Social Contract with Parents," Ms. Fisher states that three decades ago, Congress created a federal vaccine injury compensation program (VICP), which gave the pharmaceutical and medical trade industries a partial product liability shield under the National Childhood Vaccine Injury Act of 1986 (NCVIA). She suggests that their goal was to restrict civil lawsuits against vaccine manufacturers and negligent doctors whenever government mandated vaccines injured and killed Americans. The article additionally reports that back in the 1970's and 1980's, parents were filing product liability lawsuits against the three drug companies selling the DPT vaccine, and also against one selling live oral polio vaccine after children were paralyzed by vaccine strain polio. Parents were also filing malpractice lawsuits against pediatricians when their babies were re-vaccinated after reacting to the previous DPT vaccine shots with convulsions, shock, high pitched screaming, and losing consciousness, which can be signs of brain inflammation or encephalopathy. The article says that over the last twenty-seven years, $3 billion in federal vaccine injury compensation has been awarded under the NCVIA. She says that now when the U.S. Court awards compensation for a pertussis vaccine injury it is appealed by the government so that financial assistance is taken away from the child and parents. In a press release from NVIC dated September 13, 2000, Barbara Loe Fisher talks about the underreporting that is being done by the Vaccine Adverse Event Reporting System (VAERS), which is a responsibility of doctors to report. She states, "We have been waiting for the FDA to follow-up on VAERS reports and then disclose and utilize the VAERS data to increase our knowledge about vaccine reactions and possible high risk factors."

Dr. Judy Mikovits, PhD., is a biochemist and molecular biologist who worked with the National Cancer Institute for over two decades. On her professional journey, Dr. Mikovits has faced character assassination and unlawful incarceration. Her compelling story can be seen on YouTube where she additionally has many posts on research information and the state of American science that everyone needs to be aware of. Much gratitude is owed to Dr. Mikovits for her ongoing advocacy for autism.

Dr. Russell Blaylock, M.D., is a retired neurosurgeon who has researched, lectured, and written books on health and the danger of vaccines for many years. He concludes a direct correlation exists between autism and vaccines. Dr. Blaylock and I have been in contact for a number of years about Stephen. In a recent email he shared his researched information about autoimmune problems that can result from vaccines. When I asked him about autoimmune reactions he stated the following in a June 2016 email: "That what is now believed is that autoimmune reactions only occur when the immune system is dysfunctional-- mainly when the two main arms of the immune system are out of balance----cellular immunity and humoral (body fluids like serum) immunity."

He explains that,

> "Basic to this concept is the Th1/Th2 balance concept. Th1 cytokine (term for proteins released by cells which regulate immune response) profile is mainly cellular immunity driven and Th2 is humoral (as stated above, body fluids like serum immunity) driven. Most autoimmune diseases are Th2 type. Vaccines all stimulate Th2 and not Th1, which is why autoimmunity is more commonly seen with vaccines. People with abnormalities in Th1 immunity to begin with are even more susceptible."

Dr. Blaylock says, "There is strong evidence that the main damage by vaccines is not autoimmune but, *immunoexcitotoxicity, which* is a word he personally coined. He further explains that, "Prolonged priming and activation of brain microglia (small neuroglial cells of the central nervous system) and recruitment of macrophages (white blood cells whose job is to destroy invading microorganisms) to the brain, both trigger immunoexcitotoxicity--which is the process that actually does the damage. Studies have shown that in the autistic brain one sees prolonged and even lifetime activation of microglia."

In his YouTube video: "How Vaccines Harm Child Brain Development," there is much detail about the long term chronic illnesses some individuals can develop from vaccines, which range from seizures, eczema, lupus, fibromyalgia, Crohn's disease, asthma, and many other medical problems. He states issues such as these can develop due to the adjuvants added to the vaccines, such as mercury, aluminum, formaldehyde, MSG, polysorbate 80, and numerous other dangerous ingredients listed on the vaccine inserts and on the internet.

In the previously mentioned video, Dr. Blaylock links the connection of Sudden Infant Death Syndrome (SIDS) with the DPT vaccine. He gives the statistical report that seventy percent of all SIDS deaths occur within two weeks of the baby receiving that specific vaccine. He says this happens because the adjuvants that are added to vaccines create overstimulation or *immunoexitotoxicity* of the microglia, which are found mainly in the brain stem and are the primary immune cells of the central nervous system. Those cells are responsible for basic vital life functions such as breathing, heartbeat, blood pressure, and other activities of the autonomic nervous system. Dr. Blaylock says that overstimulation of the microglia causes them to overreact by pouring out inflammatory chemicals called cytokines, (chemicals produced by cells that act on other cells to stimulate or inhibit their function), which secrete toxins that suppress a baby's breathing following the vaccine. He clearly reports that SIDS is a vaccine triggered death.

One topic reported on in Dr. Blaylock's video is that in many cases of children involved in outbreaks of disease in the United States, ninety percent of those children are vaccinated. Also, that the rubella (German measles) vaccine can cause arthritis, and seventy-eight percent of doctors refuse to take it because they need to use their hands. He reports that the Hepatitis B vaccine was developed for prostitutes, but is now given to newborns. Hepatitis B is reportedly transmitted by blood, semen, or by other infected bodily fluid. Sharing needles, razor blades, or toothbrushes is another possible means of transmission, and infected mothers can pass the disease on to their newborn children. The question remains why every newborn baby is given the vaccine as standard procedure?

Dr. Blaylock also says in his video that Pneumococcal (pneumonia) vaccines protect against seven strains, yet ninety strains exist. He believes the Tetanus is the most ridiculous vaccine ever invented, and says the chance of getting Tetanus is less than getting hit by a meteor. More information is available in his videos about vaccines that people should be willing to hear, and then do more research on their own. Wikipedia supports some of Dr. Blaylock's information by reporting that, acute inflammation in the brain is characterized by rapid activation of the microglia and that over time the chronic inflammation causes the degradation of tissue and of the blood brain barrier.

I encourage every parent to watch Dr. Blaylock's videos. He emphasizes how doctors are pressuring parents into vaccinating their children by telling them to get out of their office if they don't vaccinate their children. He says the medical profession is scheduling 150 vaccines to eventually be mandated, and if that is allowed, we are facing a future where the American health will deteriorate rapidly due to vaccines. Recently, after listening to Dr. Suzanne Humphries report on SV-40 that is in polio vaccines, and reading about the danger of it that she reported on in her new book, *Dissolving*

Illusions, I contacted Dr. Blaylock to ask what he knew about this topic. He answered, sharing the following information:

"The latest results of carefully conducted tests for SV-40-linked cancers indicate that the virus is strongly associated with mesotheliomas, bone cancers (osteogenic sarcomas), ependymomas of the brain and lymphomas (non-Hodgkin's type). Over the years, a number of studies have found no correlation of SV-40 contamination and mesotheliomas, but more recent, better conducted studies have shown that many of these tests were inaccurate and missed known infections. Three independent scientific panels have concluded that there is compelling evidence that SV-40 is present in some cancers and that it contributes to their pathogenesis. Of great concern is the finding that SV-40 is strongly associated with non-Hodgkin's lymphomas, especially diffuse, large cell B-lymphomas. Lymphomas are one of the fastest growing malignancies in terms of incidence in those under age 35 years. Vertical transmission of the virus may explain this association with parents vaccinated with SV-40 contaminated polio vaccines. There is also evidence that some polio vaccines were infected with the SV-40 virus after 1961, when we were assured the vaccines were free of the virus by manufacturers."

In an article from Health Impact News, "Every Vaccine Produces Microvascular Damage," dated January 3, 2015, the author, John P. Thomas states that his intent is to preserve the contribution of Dr. Andrew Moulden, M.D., PhD, who died unexpectedly in November 2013. The author describes Dr. Moulden as a forward thinking pioneer, who worked to explain the truth about vaccine damage. He said, "Dr. Moulden understood that vaccines and toxins (in the air, in our water, in our homes, and in our food) were producing a syndrome of closely related illnesses."

The article lists a spectrum of diseases that the doctor called, "Moulden Anoxia Spectrum Syndromes," such as learning disabilities, autism, food allergies, idiopathic seizures, and others. Dr. Moulden posted a YouTube video, "Vaccine Health Truth Tolerance Lost," in which he reports on ischemia (impaired blood flow), due to clumping of red blood cells, which he says is caused by infectious pathogens in vaccines that results in cell death, and an impaired immune system. In the video Dr. Moulden made a comparison between himself and Christopher Columbus by saying that his new research on vaccines was ridiculed in the same way that people discounted Columbus who believed the world was round and not flat. Eventually, Columbus was proven to be correct.

It's amazing to me that when I try to share information on vaccine injury with others, their response will so often be, "But what about polio?" In an article called, "Vaccinations, Flu Shots and Your Immune System," posted by Dr. John Bergman, DC., under the section called Vaccination History he quotes the following, "1976 Dr. Jonas Salk, creator of the polio vaccine, says that analysis indicates that the live virus vaccine in use since the 1960's is the principal cause of all polio cases since 1961."

Additionally, on an internet site called Collective Evolution, they report that, "Six New England states reported increases in polio one year after the Salk vaccine was introduced, ranging from more than doubling in Vermont to Massachusetts' astounding increase of 642 percent; other states reported increases as well." During 1962 U.S. Congressional hearings, Dr. Bernard Greenberg, head of the Department of Biostatistics for the University of North Carolina School of Public Health, testified that not only did the cases of polio increase substantially after mandatory vaccinations- a fifty percent increase from 1957 to 1958, and an eighty percent increase from 1958 to 1959- but that the statistics were deliberately manipulated by the Public Health Service to give the opposite impression.

On a personal note, after witnessing Stephen's severe reaction to vaccines, I had hoped for many years that my thirty-three-year old daughter Laurel had escaped injury from them, but I was wrong. She is currently on medications to cope with extreme anxiety and panic attacks. Originally I thought her medical problems were simply a result of her daily exposure to our chaotic lives due to her brother's behaviors and seizures. I was hopeful that she had somehow escaped vaccine injury. However, the more I learn about vaccines, and information on vaccine injury reported from medical doctors, a link to her current health problems can be made to vaccines.

In addition to her anxiety, Laurel is now diagnosed with mastocytosis, which means she has an overproduction of histamine in her body. Histamine is produced in mast cells, which are a type of immune cells. The overproduction of those cells results in Laurel having severe allergies to inhalants and most foods. She is both gluten (wheat) and casein (milk) intolerant. Over the years, like her brother, she has been treated repeatedly for sinus, ear, and bronchial infections. She suffers daily with stomach pain, weight loss, general digestion issues, joint pain, seizures, panic attacks, PTSD, depression, severe anxiety, eczema, and was recently diagnosed with schizophrenia.

She is currently under the care of an allergist, neurologist, and psychiatrist who prescribe the following medications:

1. Keppra - to help control seizures
2. Klonopin and Xanax - for anxiety and panic disorder
3. Cromolyn - for mastocytosis
4. Seroquel - for schizophrenia
5. Carafate- for severe gastritis
6. Diflucan - for gastrointestinal issues

Laurel's doctor has tried several medications for her schizophrenia, which she has had adverse reactions to, until the most recent one, Seroquel. Laurel's diet is very restricted, which makes it difficult to find foods she can eat that will not make her symptomatic.

She takes supplements in addition to the prescribed medications to help her make it through the day. I recently found two supplements that are helping her. One is deglycyrrhizinated licorice (DGL), which is reported to help with many digestion issues. Spirulina, which is a prebiotic and natural algae that is very high in protein, is another supplement that is helping. It contains proteins, essential amino acids, antioxidants, vitamins, and trace minerals. Unlike probiotics, which are live bacteria that replace good digestion bacteria, prebiotics work to fertilize the digestive tract so that the probiotics Laurel takes can do their job more effectively.

In addition to taking a prebiotic supplement, Dr. David Perlmutter, M.D., reports that prebiotics can be consumed in foods like jicama, garlic, artichokes, and onions. Laurel's digestion issues severely affect her mental state, and the new supplements appear to be helping her with better brain function, seizures, and stomach pain.

I was invited back for the second year to speak at Oklahoma University Medical School, to a group of second-year psychiatric residents. I shared with them information about autism and my thirty-five years of experience with Stephen. My talk included information on the growing findings that the digestive tract is now referred to as the second brain. I told them when someone like Stephen is having behaviors it is not always a psychiatric problem, but is most likely a physical problem that needs to be addressed. I discussed Stephen's trip to the county jail in 2010 from their teaching hospital, and how I believe it happened because so many doctors are not recognizing the correlation between digestion and mental issues.

I suggested that when they graduate and begin practicing, always listen carefully to what the parents of autistic children are reporting and consider that the behaviors of the autistic child may be physical and not always psychiatric. I briefly shared with them the story of Alex Spourdalakis, who was a thirteen year old autistic boy who was having severe behaviors and outbursts. It was finally determined by a pediatric gastroenterologist, Dr. Arthur Krigsman, M.D., that Alex was suffering with serious intestinal issues that were causing Alex a great deal of pain. Alex was nonverbal, and as a result of the pain he was experiencing and since he was unable to express his discomfort, he would attack his mother. His mother had been asking for help with her son for years and finally reached a breaking point. With no help in sight, it resulted in the mom killing Alex, and she then attempted to take her own life. As a visual effect, I held up the DVD of Alex's story produced by Polly Tommey and Dr. Andrew Wakefield, MB, BS, FRCS, FRCPath, titled, *Who Killed Alex Spourdalakis?* I will discuss Alex's story in more detail in the next chapter. Dr. Wakefield is also an academic gastroenterologist and has published over 130 original scientific articles, books, chapters, and scientific commentaries. One of Dr. Wakefield's more widely known publications is his very informative book, *Callous Disregard.*

The future doctors listened intently as I discussed the video, and some nodded their heads as if they totally understood and had empathy for what happened to Alex. I'm sure that what I told them is not something they will normally hear in their daily medical school lectures. Hopefully, what I discussed will make them understand the importance of listening to parents and investigating ways to find answers for families, rather than just prescribing medications and housing patients in a psychiatric hospital.

Families like mine, who are caring for their vaccine-injured, and chronically sick children, currently have to rely on some prescribed medications, but additionally seek out good supplements, and make sure their children consume healthy non-GMO foods. Due to the current state of limited medical care for children like mine, parents must continue to hope, cope, and pray for more answers for their future. My family will definitely never consider vaccines in the future, and I will continue to share with others what I have learned about them. Please remember to check with your doctor before trying any of the supplements or therapies I discuss in this book.

CHAPTER 7

Raising Awareness and Problem Solving

I wish I had known thirty-five years ago what I know today about the toxic adjuvants that are in vaccines. Recently, a senior researcher from the Centers for Disease Control (CDC), Dr. William Thompson, PhD., phoned scientist and autism parent, Dr. Brian Hooker, PhD., to report that the CDC had been covering up evidence for years that provided the link between the measles, mumps, rubella vaccine (MMR), and the increasing numbers of children being diagnosed with autism.

Based on Dr. Thompson's information, a producer, Del Bigtree, along with Polly Tommey, an autism parent, produced a documentary, *Vaxxed*. The director of the movie is Dr. Andrew Wakefield. The *Vaxxed* team is currently traveling the entire country in a motorhome, from which they are meeting, filming, and documenting stories of families who have vaccine-injured children as well as families of healthy unvaccinated children. If you go to wearevaxxed.com, a Facebook page will display where the stories that they are recording can be viewed. In addition to the information the *Vaxxed* team is sharing through recorded interviews, they are also selling merchandise on their home page. The money they take in goes to further their mission to help raise awareness. Some of their merchandise includes bracelets, hats, shirts, jackets, DVD's of the movie *Vaxxed*, and other items. The money received in sales also helps to fund their travel expenses and equipment as they go from city to city across the nation. If you scroll down on the Vaxxed FB page and click on "VAXXED Nation Tour", http://www.vaxxed.com/ a site will display where you can share your personal story or experience of vaccine injury. There are videos on the site of interviews with parents, doctors, nurses, homeopaths, therapists, and siblings, who are sharing remarkable and amazing stories. Uploading the periscope application allows viewing some of these recorded interviews, as well as live interviews. The *Vaxxed* bus is covered with thousands of names of vaccine-injured children and adults. Stephen is number 905. The interactive and informative *Vaxxed* website provides crucial information, peace of mind, and doorways for those in search of answers.

Actor Robert De Niro, who heads the TRIBECA film festival in New York City, was planning to allow the movie *Vaxxed*, to be included in the 2016 film festival, but due to the controversy and backlash about the film it was pulled at the last minute. Mr. De Niro is the father of a son with autism. He has stated in subsequent interviews that he does believe that the *Vaxxed* documentary needs to be accessible for everyone to view in order for people to become informed about this complicated issue. Investigation of some of the reported damaging toxic adjuvants contained in vaccines may inspire people to think twice about vaccine safety. The lists I have seen contain a host of frightening things such as mercury, aluminum phosphate, formaldehyde, aborted fetal DNA, bovine cow serum, antibiotics, MSG, acetone, polysorbate 80, and SV-40.

Parents need to be asking questions surrounding the vaccine controversy, and be willing to listen and read stories of reported vaccine dangers. Only then will they be able to make an informed decision as to whether or not they want to vaccinate their children. Reportedly, adjuvants not only cause autism, but a lengthy list of physical problems like asthma, allergies, auto-immune disorders, cancer, diabetes, eczema, and more.

Children who end up on the autism spectrum are faced with many lifelong problems to address. One is how to provide safe, appropriate places to reside when parents are no longer able to provide care; this is especially a concern for those who are medically needy and severely challenged. Without parental oversight, or guardians to ensure that proper care and facilities are in place, many could be neglected and some may die due to lack of appropriately trained staff to meet their needs.

Even though Stephen is still living at home under our watchful eyes, there have been times when I have had to remind workers, who are paid by the state to assist him several hours per week, that their job is to care for

Stephen, not watch TV or talk on a cell phone. People who show kindness toward people with autism are essential for autistic children and adults to thrive. I have heard stories and news reports of individuals like my son being abused and neglected in group homes. In our state many facilities have been closed for various reasons, due to abuse and unsanitary living conditions, or maintenance issues. The solution to this always comes back to the need for enough funding to build suitable facilities and homes and to ensure that they are well maintained and adequately staffed. Additionally, the requirements and standards for people working in the facilities must be set very high to protect vulnerable populations. These are not unattainable goals. Enough money, whether it is obtained from private funds, state, or federal funding, needs to be dedicated to this issue to solve it. I believe that if more people understood how great the need is for this rapidly growing population, people would come forward with ways to make it happen.

For many years I have recognized the need to organize a nationally televised telethon for autism that would provide a perfect opportunity to help the general public gain a better understanding with what families of autistic people have to cope with on a day-to-day basis. Seeing children and adults with autism would help people who are not affected by autism gain a sense of how challenging living with autism is. Autism is the number one childhood disability and touches many lives. Any form of help for these children and their families should be a priority. Many people are not aware that autism surpasses all childhood cancers and Downs Syndrome, and bringing this information before the public by way of a national telethon that would allow families to tell their stories would inspire people to come forward and offer help, once they understand the need.

Having good resources in place for autistic children would help to alleviate the fears that many parents have for their autistic children's futures. "What will happen to my child when I am gone?" I have heard it stated many times in interviews with parents of an autistic child. It's becoming more frequent for me to receive emails and phone calls from mothers asking me this question, which is understandable because it is a realistic concern.

Sadly, cases have occurred where a parent has felt so desperate about this issue that they have actually killed a disabled child and taken their own life or go to prison to avoid leaving their child behind and alone when they die. Unfortunately, these tragic stories are not always reported in the news. I mostly hear about them through people in the autism community and on Facebook.

In Chicago, in June of 2013, a fourteen year old, nonverbal young man named Alex Spourdalakis was murdered by his mother and god-mother. The two women then tried to kill themselves, but survived. I reported in chapter 6 how I shared Alex's story with a group of second year psychiatry residents, because I felt they needed to hear his story and the desperation some parents face. Alex was a highly aggressive young man who had been diagnosed by a gastroenterologist, Dr. Arthur Krigsman, M.D., with small lesions in his stomach that were causing him a lot of pain. Due to his severe pain, which he could not verbalize, Alex was attacking caregivers. Eventually, his mother and godmother stated in a suicide letter that they just couldn't deal with Alex's aggression any longer, and because he was suffering so much they simply wanted to end his misery. They had repeatedly tried to get medical help for Alex.

From my experience with teaching special education and dealing with my son, I know that behavior is communication, and when children on the spectrum are unable to report what is going on with them emotion-ally or physically it can manifest as violence. I remember how horrified I was when the news story about Alex broke. The documentary about Alex is now available on DVD. At the New York City Film Festival in 2014 Alex's story was voted "Best Documentary." Dr. Wakefield had been advocating for help for Alex and his family prior to his death.

I had the great privilege to speak with Dr. Wakefield when he con-tacted me a few years ago about the video he and Polly Tommey were planning to make about Alex. He said that Polly had asked him to call and let me know that they were raising funds to make the documentary and wanted to know if I could help with fundraising. I told him I would send them what I could to help out, and would additionally contact news stations to see if they might be willing to share Alex's story and post an address to which contributions toward making the video could be sent. Unfortunately, none of the stations I contacted called back to offer help on Alex's story. However, I am pleased that through the efforts of Dr. Wakefield and Polly Tommey, the film was completed to share this tragic story. I've listened to comments from people who saw the documentary about Alex, and they reported how deeply moved they were by it. At the end of the DVD some of the comments of people leaving the theater after seeing the film were, "Doctors need to listen to parents," "We have a broken medical system," and, "Our current health system is failing us." One comment I really took note of was, "Everyone is touched by autism." Recently, Dr. Wakefield reported that instead of Alex's mother being charged with murder, and facing time in prison, she has been released, which was very good news.

When I watched the video about Alex's story it brought to mind many striking similarities of what we have been through with Stephen. He has been strapped down to a bed and denied needed medical intervention many times. Parents of children like this are not being unreasonable in asking for help for their children. It's a very hard life, not only for the parents, but for the child who is suffering.

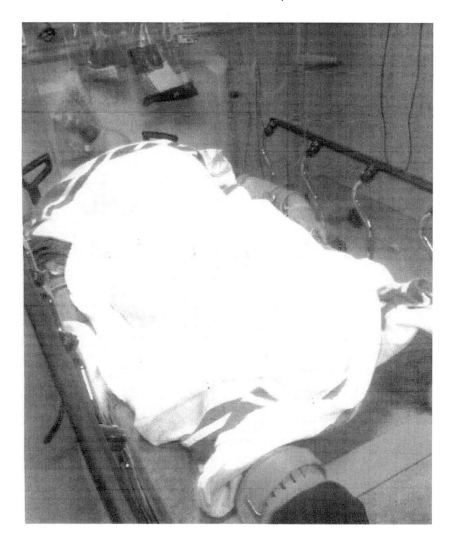

For example, the five ulcers Stephen had in 2012 that went untreated for seven months and caused him to lose seventy-seven pounds. He could not keep food down and was no doubt suffering great pain from the ulcers. Wouldn't it have been nice if Stephen could simply have told us the reason he was unable to eat and keep his food down? Unfortunately, Stephen's limited expressive language did not allow him to say, "Mom, when I try to eat, my stomach really hurts." Like Alex, and so many other children with autism, Stephen suffered in silence because of medical neglect.

Another area that needs to be addressed in support of our children is better training for police and first responders to situations where an autistic person is having a meltdown. In some police forces they are beginning to train crisis intervention team officers to be first responders. These officers have been taught to understand the violence that some people on the spectrum can exhibit, and that their violence may have an underlying medical cause, versus choosing to be violent or non-cooperative. Without proper training in place for professional emergency services workers, a call for help for a person with ASD could turn deadly. This needed training is close to my heart because police officers have been called to our home, sometimes multiple times in a twenty-four-hour period, due to Stephen's violent outbursts.

I have spoken to groups of police officers and first responders about what to expect when they arrive on the scene involving a person with autism. I emphasized to the officers that people like my son are not acting out because they choose to act that way, they are simply victims of their own disability. In Stephen's case, when he has a meltdown, it's usually because he in pain and needs a medical evaluation or medication adjustment for seizure activity. On many occasions after Stephen's encounter with police, and after his medication takes effect, he will cry and say, "I'm sorry officers, please shake my hand." He then repeats over and over, "I'm sorry momma." It makes me so sad to hear him apologize for something that is not his fault, and I always reassure him that it's okay.

When Stephen was still able to walk, there were times when the police would arrive and he immediately charged the officers, along with name calling, cursing, kicking, hitting, and trying to bite them. When this happened, Stephen didn't stop, and the officers had no option but to handcuff him and sometimes shackle his feet. As the officers would begin arriving after the 911 call, I would always quickly begin to explain to them that Stephen was having seizure activity that brought on his aggression. It's extremely difficult, as a mother, to watch your child in such a state, being handcuffed on the floor and screaming. Not to mention the numerous abrasions and injuries he has suffered over the years during physical battles with police. On one occasion he ended up with a broken thumb and multiple rug burns to his face after a confrontation with police.

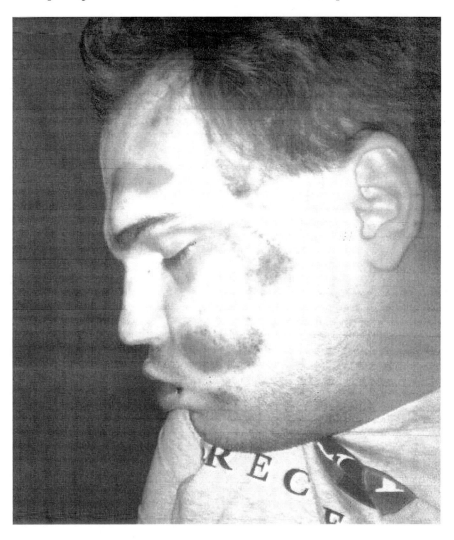

Stephen's seizure disorder can literally cause him to have hundreds of seizures a day, and almost always triggers aggression. Most of his seizures are very brief absence seizures or drop seizures, which can cause him to lose his balance and fall. Stephen's violence from seizures and accompanying adrenalin rush can change the appearance of his eyes dramatically.

His pupils can dilate during an episode so that the iris disappears, and his normally blue eyes appear to be very dark brown. When Stephen was taken to jail in 2010, his eyes were so dilated that they listed his eye color in the mug shot as brown. During Stephen's aggressive episodes there is no reasoning with him, and he looks like a frightened, cornered, wild animal. When he is in that state, nothing calms him down, the only choice is to call the police and give Stephen PRN medications.

Inmate Query

Booking Detail.

NAME:	PUCKETT,STEPHEN	
DOB:	9/11/1981	
Race Code:	W	
Sex Code:	M	
Height:	5'09"	
Weight:	240 lbs.	
Hair Color Code:	BLK	
Eye Color Code:	BRO	

Photograph date **4/5/2010**

Booking Number	Booking Date	Arresting Agency Code
130438103	04/05/2010 06:10 pm	OUHS

Case Number	Charge	Description	Bond Amount
TMP0614283	ASSAULT AND BATTERY UPON A POLICE OFFICER (FELONY)	Cash or Bail	$8,000.00

Click here to register for notificiation on any changes to this offender's custody status.

I will never forget the first time that officers came to our home and had to tase Stephen. It was absolutely heartbreaking. The officers kept asking Stephen to settle down and stop charging them, and they warned him that they were going to have to tase him. Before he was tased, an officer said to me, "Mom, you want to step out of the room." I quickly refused the offer and said that I was not going to leave him. When they finally did use the taser, everyone in the room was shocked at Stephen's reaction. He was so disoriented from the seizures that the taser hardly fazed him. When the shock from the taser hit him, he simply looked down at the two wires, connected to hooks that penetrated his stomach, then backed up, sat down in a chair, and said, "OW." Stephen then proceeded to pull out the curved metal pieces that looked like fish hooks. I had never witnessed someone being tased, and it was not something I never thought would happen to my child. The officers were very surprised that he was not reacting to the pain from the electric shock. They said it had to have been painful.

After pulling the hooks out, Stephen got back up and charged the officers again. The officers responded by tasing him two more times, with the same results. Each time he just reached down, pulled the hooks out, and started going after the officers again. After the third tasing the officers said they were going to need to call an ambulance and take Stephen to the hospital for an electrocardiogram (EKG). They explained that because Stephen had been tased three times consecutively, they were required by law to take him to the hospital to make sure that the tasing had not affected his heart. They eventually managed to take him down to the floor, handcuff him, and get him loaded into an ambulance. Needless to say, it was one of the most upsetting days of my life.

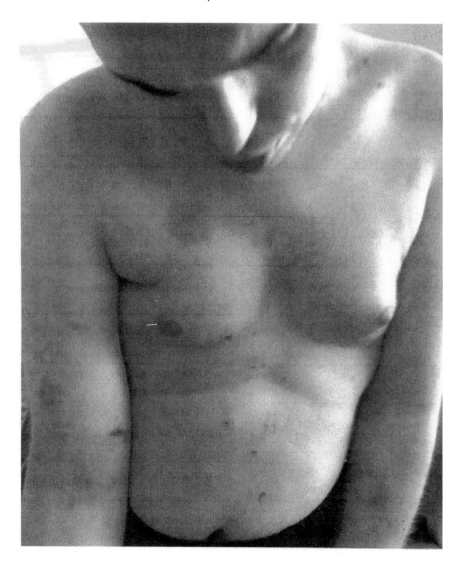

I have seen videos on television of very large men being tased and taken down on the first hit, and their immediate reaction was falling to the ground quivering and shaking. Stephen's reaction was not normal because during those violent episodes his neurological system is in such a dysfunctional state that his brain is apparently not able to report what is happening to him. The look on his face was like that of a deer in the headlights. Stephen still has six scars on his stomach from what happened that day.

Historically, when we have transported Stephen by ambulance to a hospital for seizures and aggression, the only thing I ever requested was for the doctors to admit him to the hospital and adjust his medications to stop the seizures so he would calm down. Doctors have told me that it usually requires a hospital setting to adjust medications, especially if they are going to abruptly discontinue any medications.

Sadly, until recent years the only thing hospitals would do for Stephen in the emergency room was to contact the Department of Human Services. Then he would be shipped off to a psychiatric hospital for medications adjustments, where he has suffered seizures, falls, and several injuries during his stay in the psychiatric wards. I agree that doctors need to be listening to the parents. Tom and I know our son better than anyone, and in recent years we have witnessed major improvements with his seizures and behavior after medications are properly adjusted.

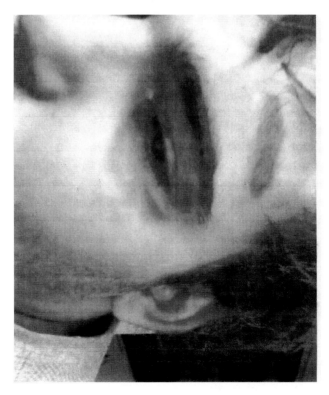

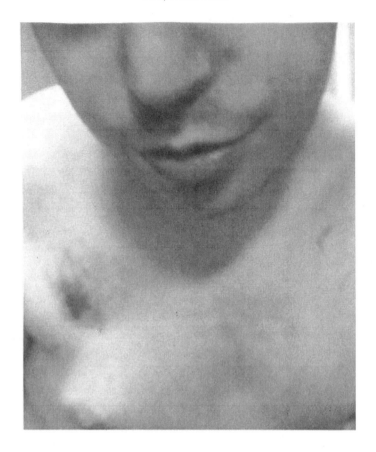

Stephen's aggression has always been connected with his seizure activity, and it's not a psychiatric issue. As previously reported, the direct correlation of his seizures and aggression has been documented in his medical records for many years.

I will be forever indebted to one local hospital that finally admitted Stephen about three years ago instead of sending him away for another psychiatric stay. The hospital emergency room doctor was not actually planning to keep Stephen in their hospital and admit him, but when they could not find beds available in a psychiatric hospital they decided to help us. Once Stephen was actually admitted and arrived in his room, the hospital called in a brilliant neurologist to make some needed medication changes. It was our first meeting with this particular neurologist, and he was the first doctor who seemed to understand what Stephen really needed. He began by explaining that Stephen was currently on six seizure medications, which he explained were way too many medications. He said that every time another seizure medication had been added, it diminished the effects of the other medications he was taking. So, more seizure medications resulted in less coverage for his seizures. He said his plan was to discontinue two of the medications that day, and he would begin titration of the other medications down to the appropriate level. He explained that this strategy is something that can be done in a hospital setting. After only two days of the medication changes Stephen was like a new person; he was very calm and pleasant. That wonderful neurologist actually helped Stephen. On a few occasions I have run into that doctor at the hospital, and I always make it a point to thank him again for helping Stephen when he so badly needed medical intervention and not a psychiatric ward.

As previously reported, Stephen's seizures began right after his first DPT vaccine at two months of age. On May 3rd, 1985, the Assistant Secretary of Health, Dr. Edward Brandt, Jr., M.D., testified before a Senate Committee, "Every year 35,000 children suffer neurological complications because of DPT vaccine." This information can be found on numerous internet locations. One source is the article I referenced on page fifty five by Dr. John Bergman, D.C. His contact information is at www.bergman-chiropractic.com.

CHAPTER 8

Exploring Services

Autism care is very expensive. The average cost of care over the life span of a person with autism can be around $3 million. In Stephen's case, for example, his expenses are high because he is medically needy. His care requires many medications, hospital stays, surgeries, ongoing doctor visits, blood tests, adaptive equipment, dental care, special foods, and supplements, some of which we pay out of pocket, such as dental care. Stephen's average cost of care is higher than average due to his diagnosis and level of functioning, but Medicare is now helping with a portion of costs because he is a disabled adult. His monthly medications alone are very costly and have at times been several thousand dollars per month. One drug he is currently taking averages about $1,700 a month.

A few years ago we pulled up at the drive-through window to pick up some of Stephen's medications. The pharmacy technician on that particular day was new, so he wasn't aware that Stephen was on assistance to help pay for his prescriptions. When the young man retrieved the refills and said, "That will be $ 1,827.50," Tom and I just looked at one another, and realized a miscommunication had occurred. Tom laughed and said, "I have the 50 cents." After a moment of silence, a pharmacist who knows Stephen and was standing nearby stepped forward and said, "I think I can fix this." We were all laughing by that time, so my husband had to add more levity to the confusion by saying, "Or, our other option is to bring Stephen over here and slide him through the service window for you to take care of him." The pharmacist laughed and said she didn't think that was a good plan.

We have learned on this autism journey that you have to find humor to keep you going.

Medically fragile people like Stephen can quickly run up the cost of health care. Another expense for Stephen is the Home & Community-Based Waiver offered through the Oklahoma Department of Disability

Services (DDS), which is a branch of the Department of Human Services. Waivered services are funded by both state and federal funds. Everyone who receives waivered services has an individual plan (IP) that is reviewed and rewritten once every year based on the individual's current needs. During the IP meeting, services can be added or removed accordingly.

Stephen's current plan includes several hours a week with a habilitation training specialist (HTS), who comes into our home and assists him with daily living skills, as well as takes him out into the community to socialize. Now that he is in a wheelchair, he can still sometimes take trips with his HTS or with his father and me to the mall to see vacuum cleaners. Additionally, he loves to go out to eat and to stores to look for George Strait DVD's.

Included in Stephen's IP are services provided by a speech pathologist that monitors his mealtime assistance plan. Stephen has been on a mealtime assistance plan for several years because he has developed aspiration pneumonia three times due to seizures while he was eating. Several years ago, on Thanksgiving Day, as our family was sitting down at the table for the dinner, Stephen took one bite of food and had a masticatory (eating seizure). He choked on the bite of food that was in his mouth. We had to call emergency help, and he was transported to the hospital. My sweet daughter had to stay behind and eat her food alone and put the remaining food in the refrigerator. Meanwhile, my husband and I had snacks from vending machines at the hospital for our Thanksgiving meal. This story illustrates how difficult our day -to -day lives are due to autism. Thousands of other families like ours have learned to cope with autism. Every holiday season I encounter people who ask, "Do you have big plans for the holidays?" Sadly, my response is always, "No, we have a child with autism."

Some of Stephen's medications make him gain weight, so a nutritionist is also provided on the yearly plan. The nutritionist's job is to make suggestions about foods to maintain good health and keep Stephen from gaining weight. The last thing he needs is to develop diabetes on top of his other medical challenges. A program coordinator (PC), who works for the agency that hires the HTS workers, also attends the IP meeting and makes monthly visits. The PC's job is to monitor the daily notes recorded by the HTS staff and make sure that everything is going smoothly. Finally, there is a case manager who coordinates all services provided on the waiver and writes the yearly IP. The case manager also makes periodic visits to our home.

When Stephen first began receiving waivered services in 2000, it was an answer to prayer because it allowed our family to have a somewhat 'normal life' for the very first time. When Stephen began going out into the community with his HTS workers, prior to him being in a wheelchair, my husband and I got a needed break. We also got more time to spend with our daughter Laurel. Trips into the community also gave Stephen something to look forward to. After graduation from high school, at age twenty-one, Stephen started attending a sheltered workshop, Monday – Friday, from 8:30 am until 2:30 pm. The HTS worker would pick him up after workshop and take him into the community before returning home.

Even though Stephen still receives waivered services, a number of things have changed in the last few years. Stephen's progressive decline, due to seizures and dependency on his wheelchair, no longer allows him to attend the sheltered workshop. However, as reported, he can still go out into the community on a more limited basis. Additionally, Medicare covers his cost for physical therapy one day a week to help maintain some of his muscle strength. A major issue that still remains with waivered services is the low pay for HTS workers; their salaries are not keeping up with cost-of-living expenses. HTS workers in our state are paid slightly over the current minimum wage. As a result, the agencies that hire the workers do not have a large pool from which to select people. Due to the low salary problems, months have gone by when we have gone without an HTS aide for Stephen.

In Stephen's case, his HTS assistant is required to provide a level of care that would at times almost equal the work of a nurse, and yet they are receiving very low pay. I have gone to our state capitol many times and met with legislators about the problem of low pay and incentives for HTS workers. I have left detailed letters explaining the need for raising disability funding in our state. The current waiting list for disabled people to begin receiving waivered services in our state is about 9,000 people. Our present governor formed a committee a few years ago to come up with a plan to shorten the waiting list. I was not asked to be on that committee, but I did attend several meetings to get a feel for what was being discussed.

At one of the committee meetings I was allowed to share my thoughts on what I believe should be a priority before moving more people onto the waivered program. I told them my concern was still the need to raise the pay for those who would be working with people like Stephen. I explained that until the pay scale for HTS workers is increased, finding enough workers who want a job with high demands is going to continue to be very difficult, especially if their clients are like my son.

Stephen is on the In-Home Community-Based Waiver, so along with the HTS in our home, his father and I serve as backup support. However, for those on the waiver who are living in direct living service (DLS) homes, also known as group homes, there are times when a worker doesn't show up, which leaves the agencies who hire the workers scrambling to find someone to cover the missing worker's shift. Worst scenario is when no one is available to cover an eight-hour shift, the case managers have to find someone to fill in for the worker in the DLS home that usually houses three clients.

One story I have heard was that a worker was signing in for an eight-hour shift in a DLS home, then leaving until it was time to come back and sign out. It's very frightening to even think about what might happen to Stephen in a setting like that. Two years ago, I invited my state senator to Stephen's yearly IP meeting because I wanted the senator to have the opportunity to listen to what is required on a daily basis to care for my son. Additionally, I wanted the senator to hear more about the issues involved in low pay for HTS workers. When the meeting ended I ask the senator what could be done to help us. The senator replied that the IP meeting was a "learning experience", and he wished more could be done to help with the needed funding. He made it clear to me that once the legislature appropriates the money for disabilities under a broad umbrella; legislators no longer have any jurisdiction as to how the money is spent. I was very disappointed to hear that, but I thanked the senator for attending the meeting.

Several years ago I took Stephen and his sister to the state capitol for a brief meeting with our governor. During the meeting I addressed the need for increased funding to help with care for people with autism and all disabilities. The governor listened politely to what I was saying, but had no response other than to frequently tell an assistant to "make a note of that."

When the meeting was over, I asked the governor if I could get a quick picture with my children. He graciously said yes, and stood up to adjust his coat and tie. When I prompted Stephen to stand up for the photo, I noticed his eyes started rolling up as he suddenly went limp and had a drop seizure. As Stephen was falling, he turned over a coffee table that was in front of the sofa where we had been seated. The seizure was brief, and I quickly scrambled to help him up from the floor and upright the overturned coffee table.

While I was handling all of this by myself, I was at the same time apologizing to the governor for the incident. The governor's response was, "Oh, that's OK Stephen, get on up here for the picture." That picture is something to behold, Stephen's mouth is hanging open, and he is drooling after the seizure, his face is pale, and he looked disoriented. After the picture I thanked the governor, and we left. About two months after that meeting, the governor signed a bill that cut disability funding by several million dollars.

The whole ordeal left me questioning where parents can turn to actually be heard and see real results that benefit their child. Getting caught up in a merry-go-round of bureaucrats has been my experience.

CHAPTER 9

What May Help

In December of 2013, Stephen was hospitalized with constant seizures. His diagnosis was encephalopathy of his brain, which MedicineNet defines as: "disease, damage, or malfunction of the brain."

When I searched information on encephalopathy, I found that it can sometimes be permanent, but in other cases the condition can be reversible, and it can be caused by a wide variety of brain disorders. Information I read on encephalopathy stated that the reversible form can be due to nutritional deficiencies, toxins such as ammonia, infectious bacteria, brain cell destruction, and other causes.

Doctors know that seizures can be a contributing factor to brain cell destruction and high ammonia levels, something with which Stephen has been diagnosed. On the website Healthline.com, I found a list of some major types of encephalopathy, and there were two types that really caught my attention. Mitochondrial and Lyme encephalopathy were of special interest to me for a couple of reasons. Several years ago, I met a woman at a national Autism Society of America conference, in Arizona, whose daughter was diagnosed with mitochondrial disorder. She explained that her daughter's condition caused her to exhibit behaviors that are very similar to autism, yet she had not received a diagnosis of autism.

When I returned home from the conference, I discussed mitochondrial disorder with Stephen's psychiatrist. I ask if the psychiatrist had ever heard of mitochondrial issues associated with autism, or had seen patients with the disorder in her practice. She said she had never heard of the association but was willing to do some investigation. The doctor did look into the matter and found a small study in a medical journal on mitochondrial dysfunction in some people with autism. More recently, I have been able to find quite a bit more information on the topic.

Medical dictionaries define mitochondria as the energy producing organelles found in nearly every cell of the human body, with the exception of a few cells such as red blood cells. When the mitochondria are not functioning correctly, it can affect many body systems such as the brain and nervous system. Muscle weakness is a reported symptom of this dysfunction, as well as muscle cramps, extreme fatigue, gastrointestinal problems such as constipation, seizures, ataxia (loss of balance), and learning delays.

One article from the Mitochondria Research Society states that some of the symptoms may be due to secondary buildup of toxic byproducts, such as ammonia. The reference to ammonia in that article caught my attention because there was a period of months when we made many trips to the emergency room because Stephen was having severe bouts with muscle weakness. The problem was so severe that I had to call firefighters to my home on several occasions to help get Stephen off the floor after he collapsed.

It always required at least two or three strong men to lift Stephen when he was in that situation because at 240 pounds, a semi-conscious person can be a lot of dead weight. The firemen were so kind to come and help with Stephen and always told me to be sure and call them back anytime I needed help. Eventually, after many trips to the emergency room for Stephen's reoccurring muscle weakness, and falling down repeatedly, the doctor suggested we check his ammonia level. She said she had been racking her brain trying to figure out why Stephen kept returning with the same issue. The doctor said it finally dawned on her that while she was in medical school they had studied the side effects of high ammonia, and one side effect is severe muscle weakness, so she ordered an ammonia test for Stephen.

When the blood test came back, the doctor was quite surprised. She said his level of ammonia was not only high, but was over the top at 172. She explained that the normal range of ammonia should be around 35. Subsequently he was started on a medication called Rifaximin, which is used to treat high ammonia levels. Now, at his regularly scheduled blood tests, to check all of his medication levels, they additionally check his ammonia level, which stays around 45. I cannot say that Stephen's high ammonia level is linked to a mitochondrial disorder, but in a report from Dr. Deepa Menon, M.D., on mitochondria disease she reports that children with ASD and mitochondrial dysfunction generate an excess of damaging byproducts in their cells.

In several other articles on mitochondrial dysfunction, one highly recommended treatment for the disorder is D-Ribose. Dr. Jacob Teitelbaum, M.D., defines D-ribose as a simple five-carbon sugar that is found naturally in the body but is not like other sugars. Dr. Jacob Teitelbaum reports that D-ribose is critical to energy recovery. The Mitochondria Research Society also reports that carnitine is often prescribed in mitochondrial disorders. After learning about the signs and symptoms of mitochondrial dysfunction, I began giving D-ribose to Stephen because he presents with many of the symptoms listed with the disorder. I had personally been taking D-ribose for several years because I felt sluggish, and it really seemed to improve my energy level. I had no prior knowledge of it being used to help people with autism. Dr. Menon says in one of her articles that the supplements L-carnitine and B-vitamin pantothenic acid (B5) are also believed to help bolster mitochondrial activity.

Lyme encephalopathy was also of special interest to me because Stephen tested positive for Lyme disease (LD) several years ago. The disease is a multi-system bacterial infection that has serious side effects and has been in the United States for many decades. We had Stephen tested for Lyme disease after a friend, who is an RN, recommended that we have him tested. She said she truly believed he would test positive, and reported that she had tested positive for LD, as had her autistic son. However, she cautioned me that in order to get an accurate test for Lyme disease, we would need to get the testing done through a laboratory in Palo Alto, California named IGeneX.

She explained that the reason for using that laboratory was because the local laboratories in our state would only be looking for antibodies. She said if a patient has had Lyme disease for a long period of time the body stops producing antibodies, which is what many labs would be testing for. The test will come back negative. She said IGeneX lab has a different approach and tests for Lyme disease by checking for certain test bands of the blood, which she stated is a more accurate way of diagnosing LD.

I contacted IGeneX lab to see what the first step was to get the testing done. They told me a kit with special packaging would be mailed to us to ensure that after the blood was drawn, it would be cooled during transport and overnighted back to them. One of Stephen's doctors wrote the order for the blood draw, and afterward it was shipped to IGeneX. Sure enough, the test result came back showing that Stephen definitely tested positive for the specific Lyme bacteria *Borrelia burgdorferi*. The unfortunate thing about an LD diagnosis is that few doctors are willing to treat patients who are suffering with it. The reason for that, I was told, is because LD is difficult to treat and very time consuming for doctors.

Within a few months after getting Stephen's diagnosis of Lyme disease, I purchased the book *The Lyme-Autism Connection*, by Bryan Rosner and Tami Duncan. They are the cofounders of the Lyme Induced Autism Foundation. The foreword of the book is written by Dr. Robert Bransfield, M.D., and states, "This book will look at some pieces of the puzzle, in particular the Lyme/tick-borne disease association with autism spectrum disorder."

Dr. Bransfield is a practicing psychiatrist in New Jersey who treats patients with LD. In a YouTube video he discusses how a certain percent of patients with LD can have anger issues, depression, anxiety, and other negative behaviors. In one of Dr. Bransfield's written articles he says that an association between LD and aggression does seem to exist in chronic patients.

The Lyme-Autism Connection brings to light the possibility of congenital transfer, with the hypothesis of whether or not Lyme disease can be passed from mother to child before the baby is born, which could compromise the baby's immune system. If that is the case it might support a need to do more research on the topic to find out why some babies are born with an unhealthy immune system and have been reported to react so violently to vaccines with dangerous toxins. This was something we witnessed with Stephen's first vaccine. The book references an article written in 1990, by Dr. John Drulle, M.D., entitled, "Pregnancy and Lyme Disease."

I highly recommend *The Lyme-Autism Connection* for its thought provoking and numerous statements from scientists, researchers, and physicians. The book additionally cites a University of California, Davis 2007 study in *The Journal of NeuroToxicology*, entitled, "Autism: Maternally derived antibodies specific for fetal brain proteins." A summary of this study states, "Your health as a mother can have an impact on your child." Rosner and Duncan quote information from a UC Davis study and say, "Autism is a physical disease, not a psychiatric disorder." This is a debate my husband and I have been proposing to doctors and hospitals to consider with Stephen for many years.

A more recent article on this topic was posted in 2013 by the Arizona Center for Advanced Medicine and Lyme. In the article, Dr. Dietrich Klinghardt, M.D., PhD, makes a powerful statement saying, "Most autistic kids have Lyme disease." This year on May 19–20th, 2017, the organization, International Lyme & Associated Diseases Society (ILADS), held a conference in Paris. Two speakers at the conference were Dr. Philippe Raymond, M.D., and Dr. Laura Alonso, M.D., who spoke on the "Treatment of autistic children with antimicrobials." Antimicrobials kill or inhibit the growth of microorganisms such as bacteria, viruses, and fungi.

Over the years we have had to use antimicrobials with Stephen for repeated bouts with candida. Some of the fungal infections were so severe that home health nurses were coming in to treat him with topical Nystatin. Stephen's compromised immune system has made him susceptible to many various infections in his life. As more and more evidence comes forward on the topic of the Lyme-autism connection, I agree with Dr. Bransfield that more research on the subject may lead to new pieces of the autism puzzle.

CHAPTER 10

Where Is the Support?

Autism is now reported to be the number one childhood disability, and quickly growing in incidence. Some believe that the incidence of autism is not increasing, and that it is better diagnosis by doctors causing the rise in statistical reports of ASD. About five years ago, I had a lengthy and civil exchange with one of our US senators about the reported increase in cases of ASD. During our conversation, the senator would not shift position that the reported increase in the number of people with autism is only due to better diagnosis, not an actual increase in the incidence of autism

Two years ago, at a town hall meeting, I had another opportunity to speak with that same senator. In an audience of several hundred people, I stood up during the question and answer segment to ask who enforces the ADA. The Department of Justice was what the senator answered. I explained that my reason for asking was because of my son's denial of medical treatment for seizures in 2010 at a local hospital, and how his denial of treatment was based solely on his diagnosis of autism. I highlighted Stephen's arrest and trip to the county jail, where his bail was set at $8,000, and he was charged with a felony assault for kicking a hospital security guard while he was having seizures. I told the senator that an I Petition had been posted about the incident, and signed by over 800 people from around the world, many of whom were parents of children with autism. Some parents who signed the petition shared similar stories of how they have been kicked out of doctor's offices because of their child's behaviors, or their child was denied medical treatment based on the diagnosis of autism. Additionally, I explained how the I Petition and signatures had been sent to the president, and I had heard nothing back about Stephen's arrest. I also held up pictures of Stephen's broken tooth and scarred wrists from the handcuffs. When I finished, the senator just looked down for a moment then responded with, "That's very sad, next question." Needless to say, I was not pleased with the senator's lack of response to my story.

I know that elected officials are always evaluating ways to cut expenditures, and perhaps, like others in positions of power, they don't want to recognize what is needed for children with autism because it can sometimes be very costly. Or they just choose to ignore what constituents tell them, and pretend that children receive appropriate medical care. Kim Stagliano is the managing editor of the Daily Web newspaper, *Age of Autism*. She is also the mother of three autistic daughters, and a great supporter of the autism community. When Stephen was arrested, I was very grateful that Kim wrote a supportive article about Stephen's denial of treatment on the blog. I have read Kim's book, *All I Can Handle/I'm No Mother Teresa*, and I totally identify with her difficult life. We need more advocates like Kim who report on these important stories on behalf of autistic children.

From 1995 to 2000, I served on the board of a local autism chapter. When I first began attending the monthly meetings, seven to ten parents showed up, when they could, based on the circumstances of their children with autism. During that five-year period, the number of parents who attended our meetings began to slowly increase. By 2000, the average monthly attendance increased to forty to fifty parents. During that period of time, outside of our small autism group, I rarely met anyone who knew much about autism. When Stephen was younger, there were times when we would be out in public and a total stranger would start questioning me about his behaviors. Some would inquire in a compassionate way, and others were merely inquisitive. The standard question would be, "What's wrong with your son?" When I would tell them he is autistic, their second question would be, "What does that mean?" Now we have a growing population of people with ASD, and instead of people asking what is wrong with Stephen, many begin telling me about their family members with autism or about a friend or neighbor who is on the spectrum. This ever-increasing population of autistic people leaves society with a desperate need for answers as to how services will be provided to serve the population, both now and in the future. Especially important for children and adults on the spectrum who no longer have parents or family members to be their voice is someone to advocate for them. Unfortunately, autism is not going to go away, which raises the big question; where will more money to meet the demands of this disability come from?

I propose that we need a national or worldwide telethon for autism to raise money for this growing population. This would not only help provide needed funding, but it would also give those not affected by autism an opportunity to listen to stories and see the children and adults who have the disorder. The money raised from the telethon could be used in many ways. It could provide more autism research, appropriate housing and medical care, respite care to help exhausted parents, daycare settings, increased training for medical personnel, teachers and paraprofessionals who specialize in autism, home modifications, medical equipment, dental care, and much more. Evening respite care would be something that could help weary parents and provide a sense of normalcy, even if it only provides an evening out for dinner and a movie once in a while.

Currently many autism chapters across the country host golf tournaments, walks for autism, and bake sales to raise money for summer camps and other various activities. The effort put forth by these fundraisers is indeed important, but we still need something on a much larger scale to meet the needs of the future projected exploding rate of autism. Sporting organizations like NASCAR, the NBA, the NFL, and others also hold fundraisers to help autistic children and raise awareness. As important as these events are, I still believe we additionally need a coordinated effort on a much larger scale.

Sadly, most families cannot afford to fund what is needed for their child with autism, and I don't know of many resources they can tap into at the present time to help them. Medicaid and Medicare programs, along with partially state-funded waivered services programs have limited funding and long waiting lists. Many children with autism need so many therapy services, such as physical therapy, occupational therapy, speech therapy, applied behavioral analysis, sensory integration services, and more. In Stephen's case we additionally have to purchase adaptive equipment for him, and make modifications to our home to accommodate his wheelchair, much of which we have had to provide out of pocket. Parents who choose to provide for their child at home, rather than place them in state care, take on full responsibility of costs. This makes it cost effective for the state and federal government because the parents are providing housing, food, day-care, supplements, outings, travel expenses for doctor appointments, and some medications not covered by Medicare.

In our situation, we also buy a dental plan to help pay for some of Stephen's dental care. When parents are no longer able to provide for their children, the financial burden falls back on the state, government pro-grams, and taxpayers to provide what is needed for a disabled person. Most parents want to have their child at home with them as long as possible, which gives the child a sense of home and family. Our home was built in the 1950's, and the rooms and hallway are just too restricting to allow Stephen to move around freely and safely in his wheelchair. We have made many modifications, removing walls and widening doorways to accommo-date that. These kinds of modifications have always been a financial strain for us, but we continue to work on what is needed for our child.

Vacations for our family, for the last thirty-five years have been totally out of the question. We have no extended family members who can care for Stephen because they have all passed away. Stephen was only four months old when my mother died, and Tom's mother died before our daughter Laurel was born. So, dropping the kids off for a visit with the grandparents was never an option.

Sheltered workshops, like the one Stephen attended after he gradu-ated high school, provided him an opportunity for socializing and a sense of self-worth. Having a job to do gave him a reason to get up each day. Stephen's daily attendance at the sheltered workshop came to an abrupt halt once he started to decline because of increased seizure activity, and he became more dependent on his wheelchair. When this happened, I received a call from the case manager at the workshop. She called to say that they loved having Stephen attend, but their limited resources did not allow them to hire an additional person to provide for Stephen's personal needs in the bathroom or to assist him with eating, which is required on his mealtime assistance plan. I told the case manager that I completely understood the workshop's dilemma, but I was truly disheartened by the call. The call meant that Stephen could not continue to attend the workshop, unless we hired someone to provide that service for Stephen, and we could not afford to do that. The current economy in our state is placing those types of workshops for the disabled in jeopardy.

Now that Stephen's requires constant around-the-clock help, and since we have no extended family, it places a lot of responsibility on my husband and me. Our daily routine includes feeding Stephen and helping him dress, shave, bathe, and transition in and out of his wheelchair throughout the day. Anyone who has cared for a loved one in this situation or who has LGS will understand how much this requires of the caregiver. When Stephen is having many seizures per day, I have often made requests to the Department of Disability Services (DDS) for double staffing for him through the waiver until we can get him stabilized. Stephen's case manager always tells me that she is sorry, but they don't have enough funding to send a second person to help us. This makes it difficult to get help with Stephen when I really need it.

However, several years ago, when Stephen was experiencing multiple seizures per day and a lot of behaviors, DDS asked me to fill out paperwork allowing them to send Stephen to live in a hospital that is about two hours away from our home. Their long-range plan was to keep Stephen in the hospital for an undetermined amount of time at the cost of several hundred dollars per day. That offer never made sense to me since funding was preventing additional staffing for him in our home. They told me that Stephen would get all kinds of therapy and help in the hospital.

When a bed finally became available at that hospital, I declined the offer. My decision was based on the fact that they would not have someone with Stephen at all times, and I knew he would try to get up from the hospital bed and fall, possibly resulting in a traumatic brain injury. Two of Stephen's medical doctors agreed that I made the right call not sending him for the long-term hospital stay. The doctors said if I had accepted that offer, it would have only been a matter of days before I would have received a call that Stephen had tried to get out of bed on his own, and was seriously injured from a fall.

Stephen was experiencing a lot of drop seizures during that time, and I knew that falling on a hard hospital floor would have been inevitable. After I declined the offer of sending him to live in a hospital, DDS was not happy about my decision. Shortly after that, I received a call from Adult Protective Services (APS) about Stephen. The caller said she could not tell me who made the complaint, but someone believed that Stephen was being neglected. She said, however, when she submitted the case to her superior, she was directed to not assign a number to the case. This meant no investigation about Stephen's "supposed" neglect would result. I know the investigation of neglect was dropped because I had already been in touch with the director of APS, several times, to report how Stephen was being neglected by the entire broken system, which included his trip to jail in 2010. The director of APS said she knew what Stephen had been put through by going to jail, and she was sorry she did not have any solutions to our dilemma.

As a result of my refusal to comply with DDS on the extended hospital stay, I received an email from a woman who had been monitoring Stephen's applied behavioral analysis (ABA) therapy that he had been receiving for several years. The email simply stated that, due to my refusal to comply with the DDS recommendation, Stephen would no longer be receiving ABA therapy. We were being punished for not complying, even though Stephen's medical doctors supported the decision my husband and I had made. In response to the email about discontinuing ABA services, I quickly replied, "Thank you for your past services for my son." My husband and I know better than anyone what is needed for Stephen, and we were not going to be strong-armed into putting his life at risk. This story exemplifies how Stephen will always need someone to take his best interest to heart and be his voice.

Every parent in this situation must do the same and continue to be vigilant about making future provisions for their child. Voice concerns to doctors, friends, and neighbors and write letters to state and federal representatives. Tell everyone who will listen what is currently needed for your child, and what your child will need in the future. Emphasize that funding is the main hurdle in getting appropriate care for someone like Stephen.

Talking with worn out parents who have spent many years fighting an uphill battle for their children saddens me. They go to bed every night concerned about their children's future. I receive phone calls from mothers crying and asking, "Mary, what is going to happen to my son, and to Stephen when we are gone?" Quite honestly, when I am asked that question, I'm at a loss for an answer, other than to tell them I'm trying very hard to get the word out. Hopefully someone, at some point, will listen and understand the need. I believe the best scenario is for individuals, maybe someone who is outside the autism community, to come forward with funding, ideas, and resources. Hopefully, continued advocacy raising awareness for autistic children will make that happen.

CHAPTER 11

People with Autism Are Valuable

Stephen can be a lot of fun at times, and I would rather spend time with him than with anyone else. Even with his challenges, he shows great depth and concern for others. Every morning when Stephen awakens, he greets us by asking, "Did you have a good sleep?" If someone sneezes he is the first to say, "God bless you." Then he asks, "Are you okay?" Anyone who spends even a small amount of time amount with Stephen quickly picks up on his sense of humor and thoughtfulness.

He loves his home and surroundings, and he never leaves the house for appointments or outings until he says goodbye to everything and everyone around him. He begins by saying, "Bye Mary, bye my house, bye my cat, bye my kitchen, and bye my dining room." As we back out of the driveway he continues with, "Bye trees, bye birds." He adds anything else he notices.

A couple of years ago two of our local police officers, who know Stephen and his history, stopped by unexpectedly to wish him a Merry Christmas. They took him by surprise because they walked in wearing their uniforms. Before they could even get the Christmas greeting out of their mouth, Stephen loudly announced, "I'm staying here." Everyone in the room, including the officers, laughed hysterically at that point. Sadly, Stephen's recall of his trip to jail in 2010 is apparently never far from his thoughts.

For many years we had a wonderful elderly neighbor, Lela, and she was considered family. Both of my children referred to her as "Gran." They did this because by the time Laurel was born, my mother and Tom's mother were both deceased. When Laurel was about three years old, she was playing outside while Lela was standing nearby. Suddenly out of the blue, Laurel called her "Gran", and it wasn't long before Stephen also referred to her in the same way. From that point on Lela always said she felt honored to be their Gran. Lela spent most of her days and evenings in our home, and we were always happy to have her here.

Anytime Lela announced that she was going back to her house, Stephen reminded her not to forget her cane, and told her to be careful and not fall down. Before Stephen was dependent on a wheelchair, he would always take Lela by the hand and walk her home. She laughingly told me several times that she had been married three times, and not one of her husbands watched over her like Stephen did.

When friends come to our home for a visit, Stephen always reminds them to drive carefully as they are leaving. People with autism are a gift from God, and society needs to recognize that. Every day Stephen will ask my husband or me to sit by him, and then he says, "I like you." We then reassure him that we love him very much. Sometimes when Tom sits next to Stephen with his arm around him, he will say, "How many dads get to hold their thirty-five-year-old son?" It's really a special time for both of them.

Stephen also looks forward to visits from his sister and always asks for a big hug. His favorite part is when she starts to leave and gives him a big kiss on the cheek that leaves an outline of her lips from a fresh application of her lipstick. Stephen asks for a mirror so that he can look at his cheek with the outline. He thinks that is one of the funniest things in the world. When Stephen first began talking at age six, conversations with him would sometimes turn hilarious when I would attempt to correct his reversal of pronouns. Understanding the use of pronouns is difficult for many young children with autism.

For example, Stephen would say, "You pick you up," meaning he wanted to be picked up. When I tried to explain to him that I am "you" and he is "me," it was always very confusing for him, and the conversation started sounding like the old Bud Abbott and Lou Costello comedy bit "Who's on First," and I would start laughing and could hardly stop. Sadly, many who live outside the autism community are not able to understand how valuable a little humor can be for caregivers. Some may even consider autistic people rather annoying if they haven't had the privilege of knowing someone with autism personally.

Many years ago, after church, we would go to a restaurant that Stephen really liked. One waitress at the restaurant always paid special attention to Stephen, and he looked forward to seeing her each Sunday. Stephen always wanted to give her a big hug and ask how she was feeling as we were leaving. One Sunday we learned that the waitress was no longer working there, but management did not give us a reason why. About one year later, when we went back to that restaurant the woman was there visiting with her former co-workers. When she saw us come in, and after we were seated, she walked over to our table and placed a small white paper sack, with writing on it, next to my plate. Then she very kindly greeted Stephen and our family. She said to me, "Read this when you have time. I can't stay while you read it because I will cry." Then she walked away. I turned the sack over and began reading what she had written. The note said, "I was a drug user for many years, and after meeting and getting to know Stephen and your family, I stopped using drugs one year ago." In the note, she said that Stephen's sweet smile and the big hugs he always gave her had impacted her life. She stated that she suddenly realized that if Stephen could handle his challenges every day, she could also rise above her dependency on drugs to deal with her own life challenges. I still have that paper sack with her testimony of how Stephen impacted her life.

I remember one upsetting comment that was posted on the I Petition about Stephen's trip to jail in 2010. A man posted the following: "Why are we wasting tax money on this useless human being who can't contribute anything to society?" That comment was hard to take. My only consolation was to recall something my wonderful mother always said when she saw individuals who were less fortunate. She would say, "There but by the grace of God go I." It's too bad that the callous man, who posted such a cruel comment, cannot summon empathy like my mother could.

People who have never had any exposure to someone with physical or mental challenges have a narrow perspective on the real world. I have always believed that it would be very beneficial for resident doctors to have early exposure to people with disabilities. Medical schools need to schedule periodic sessions with panels of parents and caregivers to come before them and share their daily struggles.

When Stephen was still in high school, my husband and I toured a sheltered workshop for people with disabilities. The man guiding us on the tour through the facility mentioned that he had one individual in their workshop who was one day a bank president, and the next day following a car accident was paralyzed and totally dependent on others. His point was that no one knows what the future holds. Therefore, we all need to learn to be compassionate, appreciative, and willing to step up and help those in need.

In Stephen's case, we are able to meet his needs at this time. My daily prayer and hope is that when his father and I are no longer are able to provide for him, an appropriate facility for Stephen will be available, where he is assured a good quality of life.

CHAPTER 12

Help and Supported Data

Stephen currently has a primary care doctor, a psychiatrist, an internist, and a neurologist who monitor his medications and health status. They have all been great support for him, and I am grateful for their care of Stephen. Additionally, over the years I have been able to acquire crucial data and recommendations from other highly qualified people in areas of medicine and research, and that data and those recommendations have benefited Stephen. Lennox-Gastaut Syndrome is a very serious progressive type of epilepsy. An epileptologist who evaluated Stephen at Cedars-Sinai Hospital complimented my husband and me by saying that we had obviously done a very good job managing Stephen's seizures because before meeting us, the oldest patient with LGS with whom he had worked had only lived to be twenty-four. The doctor's comment lends support to our personal belief in the importance of taking supplements and eating healthy non-GMO foods to maintain good health.

Dr. Russell Blaylock, M.D., is a retired neurosurgeon who has played a major role in sharing information to help us manage Stephen's health in recent years. When I contact Dr. Blaylock, he is always willing to share his latest research information and make recommendations on supplements we can try with Stephen to help maintain better seizure control.

In 2013, Stephen was hospitalized and diagnosed with encephalopathy. He was extremely weak and sleeping most of the time. Doctors caring for him at the hospital were very concerned about his condition. His neurologist stood at his bedside asking, "Stephen, do you know who I am?" "Stephen, can you open your eyes?" He could not respond to her but would at times open his eyes, just slightly, without focusing on anyone. His eyes would just roll upward and remain in that position for a brief time. Then after a few seconds, he would gently close his eyes and appear to be sleeping. However, we could not wake him up by talking to him or gently rocking him in the bed. In desperation, I contacted Dr. Blaylock and asked if he had any suggestions of what we could try with Stephen, and to my surprise he answered back in one hour.

He said he was very sorry to hear about Stephen's condition, and he gave me a link on Amazon to order a product called Baicalin, by LiftMode. He explained that Baicalin is a flavonoid and would not interfere with any of Stephen's current medications. It could stimulate brain healing, take down inflammation in his brain, and reduce seizures. His directions were to mix one small scoop of Baicalin powder with coconut oil or extra virgin olive oil and give it to Stephen twice a day. I had never heard any medical doctor state that anything could stimulate brain healing. To the contrary, I had always heard that once brain cells are damaged, they die and are not replaced.

When I shared the email from Dr. Blaylock with Stephen's neurologist, she said it might be a good idea to order the flavonoid and try it. I asked the neurologist if she had ever heard a medical doctor state that anything could heal the brain. Her answer was "No." When Stephen came home from the hospital, he was still sleeping a lot and was unresponsive most of the time. He just lay on the sofa all day, not talking, but sometimes he opened his eyes and glanced around the room, just as he had been doing in the hospital. Home health nurses began coming in daily to use catheters to make Stephen urinate.

On Stephen's first day at home I began giving him Baicalin as directed by Dr. Blaylock. I put a scoop of it in a teaspoonful of coconut oil and slipped it into his mouth twice a day. It sounds unbelievable, but after only two days of giving Stephen the flavonoid, he suddenly sat up and said, "I want my iPod. I want to play some games." Needless to say, I was very shocked and so was his HTS who also witnessed the amazing abrupt change in Stephen. What we witnessed with Stephen, reminded me of the story of Pinocchio coming to life as a real boy. It was a very joyful moment.

Stephen had a follow up appointment with his neurologist about one week after his hospital release, and his marked improvement also took her by surprise. As she walked into the exam room, Stephen was sitting up, alert, and gave her an enthusiastic, "Hi doctor." She was a bit stunned at the quick reception and replied back to him, "Hi Stephen, what have you been up to?" His answer was, "Listening to George Strait." The doctor then said, "Oh, I love George Strait." Then she turned to me and said she couldn't believe the change in him. I told her we couldn't believe it either, but we were happy about the huge improvement with him.

When I reported Stephen's improvement to Dr. Blaylock, he was also very pleased. However, he did caution me that Baicalin can chelate iron from the blood and tissues, and he suggested that we request that his neurologist order a blood test about every two months to check Stephen's iron levels. Since starting Baicalin, a couple of blood tests have reported a slight drop in his iron level. We have reduced the amount of Baicalin Stephen gets per week, which help bring his level back up, and he is temporarily on an iron supplement.

We had a brief period; right after Stephen started taking Baicalin, where we additionally added a few other supplements for seizure control. Shortly after adding the new supplements, Stephen began sleeping most of the day and was showing very little interest in computer games and other daily activities. I reported the change to his neurologist, and she ordered three days of telemetry at home to see if he was having more seizures because we were seeing some brief drops. After telemetry the neurologist reported back with the results. She said it was good news and bad news. She explained that the drops we were seeing were not seizures, but were a result of the encephalopathy. She said the good news was it appeared that the recent increase of his Depakote to 3000 milligrams per day, along with the supplements Dr. Blaylock suggested, appeared to be doing the job of stopping the seizures.

When I shared the neurologist's report with Dr. Blaylock, he said since the supplements had reduced his seizures, his high dose of Depakote was possibly suppressing his brain function, which may be presenting as encephalopathy. He suggested that I talk with the neurologist about slowly reducing his increased dose of Depakote.

When I forwarded Dr. Blaylock's email to Stephen's neurologist, she answered back saying she completely agreed that his encephalopathy was likely due to the high doses of multiple medications, and she was ready to tackle whichever one we wanted to bring down the dosages. Once Stephen's medications were adjusted, he was back on track. LGS requires a lot of juggling to maintain Stephen's appropriate medication levels to support his ability to function every day. It's really a tough disease to manage, and I hope future research will find answers for people like Stephen who are diagnosed with this difficult form of epilepsy.

Dr. Blaylock is now retired, but he remains active in different capacities of research, teaching, and lecturing, plus answering questions from parents like us, which is greatly appreciated. He ends every email with, "I will continue to pray for you and your dear son," or, "Keep me informed of his progress." I have rarely talked with doctors who have taken that much interest in Stephen's well-being.

Dr. Stephanie Seneff, PhD., is a senior research scientist at MIT. In June of 2013 I reached out to her after a friend sent me a link to one of her YouTube videos in which Dr. Seneff discusses sulfur deficiencies linked to autism. Her information in the video caught my attention, so I emailed her about Stephen. The next day I had an email response from her. Dr. Seneff said she suspects that Stephen is extremely deficient in sulfate, and she recommended feeding Stephen eggs, oysters, clams, mollusks, crabs, lobster, and scallops, which are sources of important nutrients like sulfur, zinc, cobalamin, choline, iron, and cholesterol. She also suggested that we add lots of garlic, onions, and cruciferous vegetables (broccoli, cauliflower, cabbage, and Brussels sprouts) to his diet. She said cheese would also be important for him, especially blue cheese. She recommended eliminating all fast food, processed food, soy protein, and high fructose corn syrup from his diet. She said soaking Stephen in a hot bath of Epsom salts would be an easy way to get sulfate into his body, by-passing the digestive system.

Additionally, she suggested probiotics to help repair his digestive bacteria. Another recommendation for Stephen was sunlight exposure to his eyes and to his skin in abundance, eliminating any sunscreen. She also said we should eliminate antiperspirants or antacids because they all contain aluminum, which is very damaging to the nervous system. Then in bold print she added, "NO VACCINES," no flu shot in particular because it contains mercury. She also advised us to avoid exposure to other toxins like bug sprays and to switch to non- fluoridated toothpaste.

In some of her videos, Dr. Seneff shares the dangers of genetically modified organisms (GMO), which are foods that scientists alter by combining the DNA of one or more organisms to produce specific genetic features. The herbicide Roundup, made by Monsanto, is a popular herbicide worldwide and contains a toxin called glyphosate, which is raising many concerns about its safety. Glyphosate is an herbicide used to kill weeds and grasses that compete with crops. Dr. Seneff reports that the grass and weeds are becoming resistant to glyphosates, which means the farmers are using increased amounts of it. Her concern is the transfer of glyphosates to humans after the toxin is absorbed through the root systems of plants, which then goes into the foods we eat.

Dr. Seneff reports that GMO's are linked to numerous problems, such as cancer, autism, immune problems, intestinal disorders, allergies, emotional health problems, hormone imbalance, skin problems, brain fog, and many more health issues. In one of her videos, Dr. Seneff explains how glyphosates disrupt the pathway for enzymes that detoxify toxins in the body. She describes how glyphosates deplete micronutrients and chelate minerals, such as calcium, magnesium, zinc, and iron, from the body and points out that it's well known that children with autism are deficient in zinc as well as sulfur.

Dr. Seneff is a contributor to a 2013 published study on autism called, "Is Encephalopathy a Mechanism to Renew Sulfate in Autism?" There is open access to the complete study on the following link: www.mdpi.com/journal/entropy. In the abstract it explains that the paper makes two claims:

> "(1). Autism can be characterized as a chronic low grade encephalopathy, associated with excess exposure to nitric oxide, ammonia and glutamate in the central nervous system, which leads to hippocampal pathologies and resulting cognitive impairment, and (2), encephalitis is provoked by a systemic deficiency in sulfate, but associated seizures and fever support sulfate restoration."

The abstract also states that

> "Several environmental factors can synergistically promote the encephalopathy of autism, including the herbicide, glyphosate, aluminum, mercury, lead, nutritional deficiencies in thiamine and zinc, and yeast overgrowth due to excess dietary sugar. Given these facts, dietary and lifestyle changes, including increased sulfur ingestion, organic whole foods, increased sun exposure, and avoidance of toxins such as aluminum, mercury, and lead, may help to alleviate symptoms or, in some instances, to prevent autism altogether."

Dr. Joseph Mercola is an osteopathic physician who is also an alternative medicine proponent. On his website, mercola.com, he has an article titled, "How Sun Exposure Improves Your Health and How Glyphosate Disrupts It." In the article he states that, "Sensible sun exposure is an important component for optimal health." He validates, "Dr. Seneff has a wealth of information in an area that many are not knowledgeable about, and that is the importance of sulfur." Additionally he quotes Dr. Seneff,

> "When you expose your skin to sunshine, your skin synthesizes vitamin D3 sulfate. This form of vitamin D is water soluble, unlike oral vitamin D3 supplements, which is unsulfated.

The water soluble form can travel freely in your blood stream, whereas the unsulfated form needs LDL (the so-called "bad" cholesterol) as a vehicle transport. Her suspicion is that the simple oral non-sulfated form of vitamin D likely will not provide the same benefits as the vitamin D created in your skin from sun exposure, because it cannot be converted to vitamin D sulfate."

Dr. Mercola's article is quite lengthy, but contains a huge amount of information based on Dr. Seneff's research, and it is worth reviewing. It corroborates everything Dr. Seneff shared with me for Stephen.

Stephen has shown significant improvement in seizure control, behavior, and alertness since we began following the recommendations from Dr. Seneff and Dr. Blaylock. I am forever grateful to both of them for their willingness to show concern to help people with autism. Dr. Seneff's website is people.csail.mit.edu/Seneff, and it has a plethora of information for parents and medical professionals as well. Her newly published book, *Cindy & Erica's Obsession*, addresses ways to solve today's health care crisis. The cover explains how the book includes information on Autism, Alzheimer's, Cardiovascular Disease, ALS and more.

CHAPTER 13

Bacteriophages

As an infant, Stephen had repeated ear, sinus, and bronchial infections that started right after he was first vaccinated. I cannot prove scientifically that there is any correlation between the infections and the vaccines he received. However, the timing of the vaccines and his infections, as well as reported vaccine injury information, lends support to my belief in the connection.

As Stephen grew older, the infections continued to reoccur, which required him to be on more and more antibiotics. After taking multiple rounds of antibiotics, he would start having bouts with diarrhea, which was very difficult to control. The doctor's solution for his diarrhea was usually to give more antibiotics. As a result of this vicious cycle, Stephen remained so sick that his doctors would sometimes prescribe long-term, low-dose antibiotics. Many times he would finish a complete course of antibiotics and within days his fever would spike, and he was sick again.

In 1990, at age nine, Stephen was still in that same cycle of being sick and taking antibiotics. My concern was always the possibility of irreversible organ damage from the over use of antibiotics. In those early years, I had never heard of *Clostridium difficile* (C-diff), which is another potential problem resulting from taking repeated rounds of antibiotics that kill off not only the bad pathogens in the digestive tract but also the healthy digestive flora. Overuse of antibiotics puts patients at risk of this deadly disease.

I contracted C-Diff in 2015 following several back surgeries, and it was so severe that my doctors did not expect me to survive. After the doctors told me my chances of surviving C-diff were not good, I remember praying and asking God to let me survive to finish this book. After that prayer, early the next morning my doctor came in to report that my most recent bloodwork indicated a very slight improvement. He said, "However, you are not out of the woods yet," but he was encouraged by the new bloodwork. Praise God, I did survive C-diff, but it took me many months to regain enough physical strength to complete this book.

During the early 1990's when Stephen was on the long-term antibiotics, I was visiting one morning with my neighbor, Lela, about my concerns about getting Stephen off of antibiotics. Lela agreed with me that I needed to find answers for Stephen, and she began telling me about a treatment that one of her doctors had used with her in the 1950's that had stopped her repeated infections. She said the treatment was a bacteriophage called Staphage Lysate (SPL). The doctor who had treated her was deceased, but his wife, who had been his nurse, was still living.

The doctor's widow lived near a friend I knew from college, and surprisingly I was able to contact her. When I called the doctor's wife and explained why I was inquiring about the phage treatment her husband had used, she quickly responded by saying that SPL was a miracle cure, but that she didn't think it was still available. She said her husband had purchased it from Delmont Laboratories in Swarthmore, Pennsylvania, and suggested I give them a call. When I contacted the laboratory a lab technician answered on the first ring. I told him the reason for my call, and he immediately said it was interesting that I should call at that time because the FDA was actually allowing human trials with the bacteriophage again. He said SPL would not only stop infections but would also boost the immune system.

After speaking with the doctor's wife and Delmont Laboratories, I called Stephen's doctor and reported what I had learned. Thankfully, Stephen's doctor was very interested in learning more about SPL, so she also made a call to Delmont. After visiting with a technician at the lab, Stephen's doctor called back to say that it sounded like something we needed to try with him. I agreed, so the doctor ordered several vials of SPL for Stephen. The cost of placing an order for a one-month supply of SPL was relatively inexpensive.

Once Stephen began receiving weekly treatment with SPL, the result was amazing. Within a short time, Stephen was off of antibiotics for the first time in many years. To this day, I believe that SPL saved Stephen's life. Unfortunately, in 1994, Stephen's doctor received a letter from the FDA stating that SPL was being taken off the market for human use; however, it is still available today for veterinarians to use in treating dogs with skin disorders. I feel extremely fortunate that my neighbor told me about SPL and that Stephen had the opportunity to receive treatment long enough to break the terrible cycle of constantly relying on antibiotics. Even after SPL was no longer available for human use, Stephen's benefit from receiving the treatment appeared to continue for several years. Today at thirty-five, he may occasionally need an antibiotic, but only on very rare occasions.

Several years ago, I made contact with a woman in Reigate, England named Grace Filby who was a science and engineering ambassador. She devoted many years to researching and promoting information on the effectiveness of using bacteriophages to kill deadly infections such as methicillin-resistant *Staphylococcus aureus* (MRSA) and Escherichia coli (E.coli). In 2007, Grace was awarded a Winston Churchill Traveling Fellowship funded by the Winston Churchill Memorial Trust. The fellowship afforded Grace the opportunity to travel to international conferences in Canada, the United States, Poland, Georgia, France, England, and Scotland, meeting leading scientists and physicians. She additionally visited clinics in the Republic of Georgia and Poland where she observed, "Dedicated doctors and nurses who were saving lives and limbs daily through their use of bacteriophages." Grace told me that she met many people at those clinics from the United States who had been told by their American doctors that they were going to die because they were antibiotic resistant.

Grace once asked if she had permission to give my phone number to a woman from Florida who she had met at a clinic in Tbilisi, Georgia. She said the woman wanted to call and share her story of bacteriophage treatment with me and hear about Stephen's use of SPL. Grace said US doctors had told the young woman she was going to die from MRSA and two other deadly infections. I told Grace to please have her give me a call.

When I received the call from the woman in Florida, we talked for over an hour. The young woman explained that she had gone into the hospital in Florida for a minor procedure and somehow developed three deadly infections. She said her doctors walked in and said she was resistant to all antibiotics and told her to get her affairs in order because she was going to die. She said they even sent in grief counselors to counsel her on the dying process. She told me that she did not accept the idea that she was going to lie in that hospital bed in Florida and die at the age of twenty-four. Instead she checked out of the hospital in Florida and flew to Phage Therapy Center in Tbilisi, Georgia. Her next statement in that conversation was, "I'm now twenty-nine years old and alive to tell my story." I told her that her story and Stephen's are both amazing and need to be told worldwide.

During Grace's fellowship, she once traveled to a wound care clinic in Lubbock, Texas, where she observed and videotaped the use of bacteriophages to treat a woman's large leg ulcer. Grace posted the successful outcome of that story on YouTube. This particular story is of special interest to me because people like my son, who are wheelchair bound, will sometimes develop pressure sores from sitting so much and not getting proper blood flow in certain areas. Those sores can turn into infections that are extremely difficult to heal. It's encouraging to know that there are phages available we could try if we are ever confronted with that type of problem. Grace devoted many years to writing and sharing her recorded experiences about the healing effects of bacteriophages. I am extremely sad to report that, as I was writing this chapter, my brilliant, wonderful, caring friend, Grace Filby, passed away. I am very happy that in recent years she received recognition for her hard work and relentless effort in getting such valuable information out to help others.

In 2008, Grace was presented the Churchill Fellows' Silver Medallion Award for her phage research by Lady Mary Soames, Sir Winston Churchill's daughter. She was so proud of that award. She shared with me in an email that the award was originally going to be presented to her by

Prince William, but he was unexpectedly called away for some type of military duty.

More recently, in April 2015, Grace was recognized by Queen Elizabeth at a reception in Buckingham Palace for her research on bacteriophages. Grace was truly a light in the world. She will be greatly missed by those whose lives she touched, for the wealth of information she shared on phage treatment, and for advocating against Human papillomavirus (HPV) vaccines. She told me that researchers have identified over 100 different strains of HPV, and the vaccine only protects against four strains. Grace was a pioneer in getting this information to the public, and several years ago she was on the streets of London with banners opposing Gardasil HPV vaccine and doing radio interviews about it. Grace also has a YouTube video posted on the danger of Gardasil and its toxins. Additionally, many videos are on YouTube of the mothers of young healthy girls who received the HPV vaccine and died or became seriously ill immediately after the vaccine.

Grace was also a contributing author in a 2012 book titled, *Women in War*. She wrote the chapter "Women Who Thawed the Cold War," which references bacteriophage treatment and Stephen's story about receiving SPL. Grace said she was so happy we became acquainted. For years she included Stephen's story of receiving treatment with SPL at her speaking engagements. She also shared Stephen's story with doctors and scientists she knew.

Several years ago, she sent me a very important paper on the history of bacteriophages. The report stated that during World War II, which was prior to the introduction of antibiotics, they would find bacteriophages in the medical kits of captured enemy soldiers from Stalin's army. Grace said that more soldiers die in battle from secondary infections than from bullets, which was the reason behind having bacteriophages with soldiers in the field. In one of her earliest emails Grace commented, "You have been sharing your experience with phage treatment in the US and I have been doing the same in Europe for many years." She commented several times,

"It's such a shame that phage treatment is not allowed as an option when antibiotics have failed someone." She also voiced her concern as to how we now have a greater need to have phage treatment made available for human use worldwide.

When I reported on Stephen's treatment with SPL in my first book I stated that my hope is that the medical community will take a closer look at the benefits of using SPL in patients who have compromised immune systems, question why the bacteriophage treatment was put on hold, and make requests that funds be appropriated to do more research on the use of bacteriophages.

In a State Health Notes Report from Pennsylvania, dated August 6, 2007, an article by Matthew Gever, "Cutting Infections Is Keystone to Health-Care Savings," says former Governor Ed Rendell signed a bill (SB 968) that required hospitals to carry out infection control plans. The article says that if by 2009 a facility complied and reduced infections by ten percent, they would receive a financial award. Governor Rendell was on a talk show several years ago addressing how the United States spends billions of dollars each year treating hospital acquired MRSA. Immediately after listening to the governor's report on this, I sent him information about phage treatment and the clinics in Poland and the Republic of Georgia. I told him about Grace and how she traveled to those clinics and met many people from the United States who were successfully treated for MRSA with bacteriophages. However, I heard nothing back from the governor.

In 2014, *Scientific American Mind* posted an article by Melinda Wenner, "Gut Bacteria May Play a Role in Autism," which says that research suggests that as many as nine out of ten individuals with autism suffer gastrointestinal problems. She says that scientists have long wondered whether the composition of bacteria in the intestines might be abnormal and drive some of the symptoms. After witnessing what bacteriophage treatment did for Stephen in the early 1990's, I will always wish for the day when phage treatment will be readily available in the United States again.

However, I'm sure that will not happen until funding for more research becomes available.

When I spoke with the doctor at Delmont Laboratories in 2007 about the possibility of getting SPL back on the market, he said he hopes that someone will come forward and make that happen because people need it. He said Delmont is a small laboratory with limited funding, and they had to pull SPL for human use in 1994 due to the pressure being put on them to do expensive clinical trials. He told me that his lab just doesn't have millions of dollars to do the research they were requiring him to do.

When I shared Stephen's positive results from SPL treatment with the neurosurgeon, Dr. Russell Blaylock, he responded that his concern is that SPL can also stimulate B-cell activity, which can worsen autoimmune disorders. Perhaps more research on SPL would find a way to avoid the possibility of any negative results.

When I asked Grace Filby about B-cell stimulation, she responded by saying, "Just to clarify, SPL is a brand name of the US product so it is not exactly the same phage product I have witnessed in Poland, USA and the Republic of Georgia, and here in the UK. However, I do put SPL under the general heading of phage therapy." She explained that in clinics abroad the doctors use many other types of phages that are specific to the bacteria they have identified. She referred to them as "phage cocktails."

In a recent conversation, the president of Delmont Laboratories, Dr. David Ganfield, PhD., stated that their product, Staphage Lysate (SPL) contains "whole phages with bits and pieces of staphylococcus aureus," which they have manufactured for years and are licensed to sell to veterinarians for use in canines. He explained that many vets have used SPL to treat staphylococcus infections due the extreme number of dogs that have become resistant to antibiotics.

I recall telling a veterinary friend of mine about SPL back in the 1990's when we were using it with Stephen during the limited human trials. He said he was going to order some from Delmont Laboratories for use in his practice. When I spoke with him a few months later, he said he couldn't believe how many dogs' lives had been saved since I had told him about SPL. He said it worked so well that some dogs, which would normally have been euthanized due to severe skin infections, were saved by the use of SPL.

Several years ago, Grace shared information on Elizabeth Taylor's reported treatment with SPL in 1961, while she was in London filming Cleopatra. An article from the *New York Times*, dated March 9, 1961, reported Ms. Taylor recovered from staphylococcal pneumonia. Her recovery was possibly due to the SPL that was overnighted to her in London from Delmont Laboratories. Information on this story is also recorded in two of Ms. Taylor's biographies, *Liz* and *Elizabeth Taylor the Last Star*.

In Thomas Hausler's book, *Viruses vs. Superbugs*, he states in the foreword that antibiotics are becoming increasingly ineffective. He says this has dire consequences for patients. He reports that because of this, the future development of new antibiotics is a big financial risk for pharmaceutical companies due to poor potential profits. However, he reports, "There are some scientists who have resumed research on bacteriophage therapy, and that's a good thing."

On HistoryofInformation.com, an account is given of the 1915 discovery of bacteriophages by English bacteriologist Dr. Fredrick William Twort at the University of London. However, the term bacteriophage was coined by Felix d'Herelle in 1917, which independently confirmed Twort's discovery.

The introduction of an article in *Bacteriological Review*, December 1976 by Donna H. Duckworth titled, "Who Discovered Bacteriophage?" questions whether d'Herelle was altogether honest in claiming to have had no knowledge of Twort's 1915 discovery when he published his 1917 work. On page 800 Duckworth concludes, "Whether or not Twort had seen the effects of phage first, it was d'Herelle that, by the sheer volume of his work, had brought the phenomenon to the attention of the world and had made research with bacteriophage one of the most exciting fields to work in during the 1920's."

A phage is a waterborne virus that kills bacteria. They are the most ubiquitous micro-organism on earth and found in seawater, soil, sewage, drinking water, rivers, inside plants, and in human and animal microbiota. The structure of a phage is interesting and varies. The best studied phage are the T4, which have a head that contains DNA, a collar, sheath, base plate, and tail fibers. Their structure always reminds me of a lunar landing module.

The word "phage" is derived from the Greek word "phagein," which means to eat. Phages can only survive on harmful bacteria and need the bacteria as a host to replicate. So once they are inside the body, they only seek out harmful bacteria without destroying natural flora, unlike antibiotics. After landing on the bacteria the phage sends down a probe or tube into the bacteria and begins releasing its own DNA, which begins to replicate, producing more phages very rapidly. Enzymes are then released and dissolve the walls of the bacteria, causing the bacteria cell to rupture or lyse. Then the newly produced phages move on to seek out other harmful bacteria in the host.

A YouTube video with Dr. Vincent Fishetti, PhD., "Bacterial Biofilms & Phage Lytic Enzymes," explains how bacteriophages cannot affect human tissue, so they are completely safe for humans. He states in the video that ten times more bacteriophages are on earth than bacteria, and that every two days half the bacteria on earth are killed by bacteriophages. He gives the history of phage treatment in the 1930's and 1940's and explains how phage therapy was the way people killed bacteria. He says in the United States in the early 1940's young pharmaceutical companies were beginning to use phage as a means to kill bacteria up until the point that antibiotics were introduced. He explained at that point the United States and the developing world stopped developing phage as a therapy and went to antibiotics. Now in his laboratory they are again looking at phage lytic enzymes as a way to control or prevent infections.

A 2009 article by Elizabeth Svoboda in *Popular Science* titled, "The Next Phage," reports on the clinic in Lubbock, Texas, where Grace Filby visited in 2007. The article discusses the patient who was successfully treated with phages for a leg wound. As the wound began to heal, she quotes the patient as telling the doctor, "You'd better take pictures of this...or nobody is going to believe it."

In reference to phages the article also states, "They prey only on bacteria, never human cells, they rarely spread from person to person, and, perhaps most important, bacteria have trouble becoming immune to them." Additionally, the doctor at the wound care center is quoted, "Phage needs to be fast tracked. It works. It's completely natural." *Prevention* magazine published a story in 2015 by Koren Wetmore, in which she reports on a woman named Laura Roberts, from Fort Worth, Texas, who had been told by doctors in the United States that she had three months to live. The article states that she was not dying from terminal cancer, but from a sinus infection that antibiotics could not cure. Ms. Roberts was quoted, "When I was told to get my affairs in order, it hit me like a ton of bricks."

Instead of accepting that she was going to die, Ms. Roberts, along with her brother, booked a flight to Tbilisi, Georgia, where she received treatment at the Phage Therapy Center. The article quotes Roberts, "I didn't know if it could help me, but if I was going to die, I was going to die fighting." The article states that samples from Robert's infection revealed three strains of MRSA. It also reports that phages completely cured her infection and that for patients with simpler cases, the center ships patient's at-home treatments of targeted phage drops, drinks, or powders legally through the FDA's personal importation policies.

I was recently in touch with the CEO of Phage International, Christopher Smith, about Stephen's skin outbreaks from folliculitis. He told me that they have had a number of patients with this condition. He said it requires treatment by a dermatologist with phage therapy experience, and that his company has an approval process through the FDA to allow shipment of phages for people in the United States to be treated for various other infections. He said the best reference is to visit their website, www.phagetherapycenter.com.

Dr. Elizabeth Betty Kutter has a PhD. in molecular biology/bio-physics and has been researching phages for over fifty years. I recommend a book on phages edited by Dr. Kutter and Alexander Sulakvelidze, PhD., published in 2004, *Bacteriophages Biology and Applications*. Dr. Kutter was a personal friend of Grace Filby. Grace always spoke very highly of Dr. Kutter and considered her an expert on phage therapy. In Grace's last email to me she was reporting how she had recently had lunch with Dr. Kutter and during their visit she shared Stephen's use of phage treatment in 1990 and his successful results from receiving SPL.

In an article by Doris Faltys, Evergreen Researcher, Dr. Kutter announces, "There's A Phage for That." She quotes Dr. Kutter, "In the Republic of Georgia, phages are being used routinely as part of general health care and are licensed to be sold in the pharmacies, approved by the government's ministry of health." Dr. Kutter says new phage batches are tested every six months in terms of efficacy and sterility. She also states that, "It's a standard part of medical practice in that part of the world. They come in little 10 ml bottles which you can buy off the shelf in the pharmacy." The article points out that in most western countries the use and research of phage therapy ended in the early 1940's because of the availability of antibiotics. She additionally states that as a compliment to antibiotics, phage therapy is currently used in a few other parts of the world and in some research situations in this country for treating diabetic ulcers, MRSA, lung infections of people with cystic fibrosis, pseudomonas, and various severe or intransigent (inflexible) gastro-intestinal problems. Ms. Faltys also reports that Dr. Kutter was on the board of the Naturopathic College in Seattle for its first fifteen years of operation and that she is known for her research on phage and her interest and enthusiasm for collaboration.

On April 1, 2013, *Pittsburgh Post-Gazette* posted a very informative article by David Templeton called, "Bacteriophages offer a way to fight resistant bacteria, but their use still awaits approval in the US." The article addresses how the CDC recently sounded a national alarm about "superbugs," which they describe as "nightmare bacteria" that are becoming untreatable to a point of killing one of every two patients whose infections reach the bloodstream. The article additionally addresses how the U.S. Food and Drug Administration require extensive research and human clinical trials before approving the safety and efficacy of a drug. This is an obstacle to developing phages in the United States because of the high cost of the research, development, and approval, which can cost up to a billion dollars, a prohibitive sum for some pharmaceutical companies, especially for a drug that would work with a single prescription One section of the article describes a 2009 clinical trial at the University College London's UCL Ear Institute and its partner, the Royal National Throat, Nose and Ear Hospital on the effectiveness and safety of a therapeutic bacteriophage in treating a chronic ear infection, otitis, caused by antibiotic-resistant *Pseudomonas aeruginosa*.

Repeated ear, sinus, and bronchial infections that require multiple rounds of antibiotics are common in autistic children. On page 449 of Dr. Suzanne Humphries' book, *Dissolving Illusions*, there is a list of vaccines from a 1972 U.S. Senate Hearing of thirty-two "worthless vaccines" that were licensed and on the market. Included on the list is Product N Staphage Lysate of type I, Product O Staphage Lysate type III, and Product P Staphage lysate types I and III. The Senate hearing reports that they were "of little value and perhaps even harmful." Staphage Lysate has been used from the early 1900's to boost the immune system. Dr. Humphries' book also states, "The more scientists learn about the immune system, the more they realize their profound lack of understanding." In 1990, Stephen's treatment with SPL quickly boosted his immune system, which broke the cycle of his chronic dependence on antibiotics. Therefore, when I read about the inclusion of SPL on the list of "worthless vaccines," I wanted to know more about the 1972 Senate report. Dr. Humphries book has a vast amount of facts on vaccine history and statistical information that I found interesting and helpful.

After I finished reading Dr. Humphries' book, I called Delmont Laboratories to inquire about the 1972 Senate list of "worthless vaccines." I spoke with Dr. Dave Ganfield, the CEO of Delmont Laboratories. He told me that the 1972 Senate list of worthless vaccines was modified in the late 1970's, and that Staphage Lysate was removed. In a book published in 1992, entitled, *Cancer Therapy*, by Ralph Moss, PhD., it is stated on page 456, "In 1975, this innovative form of immunotherapy (SPL), was quietly removed from the ACS (American Cancer Society) unproven method list." This was encouraging to hear, but notice how SPL was quietly removed. During my conversation with the doctor at Delmont Laboratories he also shared a story with me about a man named Charles Tobey Jr., whose life was saved from cancer with SPL treatment many decades ago. I found the story amazing. Mr. Tobey was the son of Charles William Tobey, Governor of New Hampshire from 1929–1931 and US Senator from 1939–1953. His son's remarkable story can be found easily online using the title "Charles Tobey Jr. Reports on Cancer and the Venal Medical Conspiracy."

Charles Tobey Jr.'s story takes place in the late nineteen forties and the outcome was miraculous. He had been told by his three doctors that he had one to two years to live because he had a vicious form of cancer. In the fall of 1948 his father sent him to Medford, Massachusetts to see a physician named Dr. Robert Lincoln M.D., who was treating patients with a bacteriophage. Dr. Lincoln had filed for a patent on his use of bacterio-phages on August 24, 1946.

Sadly, Mr. Tobey reports in his article that men like Dr. Lincoln, and others who try to help mankind, get kicked in the stomach and knifed in the back by the un-American Medical Association. After Mr. Tobey received treatment for his cancer from Dr. Lincoln, a Concord physician ordered an x-ray of Mr. Tobey, hoping to find that Dr. Lincoln had not done a good job. Surprisingly, the x-ray did not show one scintilla of any cancerous tissues.

Mr. Tobey states that, "As a result of Dr. Robert Lincoln's use of SPL to successfully treat many patients with cancer, his medical license was withdrawn by the Massachusetts Medical Society in 1952. Remember how Dr. Andrew Wakefield was treated so unjustly, and also had his license to practice taken away? He was accused by the General Medical Council (GMC) in the United Kingdom of linking vaccines and autism. Based on his research as an gastroenterologist he wrote a paper, along with twelve other author's that was published in Lancet in 1998. The authors claimed to have identified a link between bowel disease, autism, and the MMR vaccine. Dr. Wakefield was simply calling for suspension of the triple MMR vaccine until more research could be done on combining the three viruses. Dr. Wakefield was simply trying to save children from becoming autistic. In Ecclesiastes 1:4-11 the Bible talks about cycles that are repeated and concludes that, evil remains an ongoing conflict in this world.

The story of Mr. Tobey's treatment with SPL was more recently recorded on March 12th, 2017 in *Truth Talk News*. In an article entitled, **Suppressed Cancer Treatments**, by Howard Nema, there is a section called, "The Fitzgerald Report" which tells how, "Charles Toby Sr. enlisted Benedict Fitzgerald, an investigator for the Interstate Commerce Commission, to investigate allegations of conspiracy and monopolistic practices on the part of orthodox medicine". It is a rather lengthy article but very informative.

Based on the information I have compiled over the years about bacteriophage treatment, and observation of Stephen's successful treatment with SPL, my hope is that researchers in the United States will re-examine the potentials of phage treatments. Researchers are beginning to take a second look at the use of bacteriophages due to the increased number of people who are becoming resistant to antibiotics. Scientists need to look at the success that clinics abroad are having with phage treatment. By taking the time to do some investigation on this, researchers may learn more about ways to incorporate the use of phage cocktails, which could prove to be life saving for children and adults like Stephen who have compromised immune systems and gastrointestinal issues.

CHAPTER 14

Moving Forward

I believe that by raising awareness about what people like Stephen need, something good will come for them. In order to achieve what is needed for people like my son, parents in the autism community must continue to unite and share new helpful data with one another, continue to inquire into new solutions, and most of all be open-minded to new information. With the incidence of autism growing exponentially, current and future information on what is needed to help these children and their families must be brought to light. We know the worldwide epidemic of autism crosses all boundaries without regard to any specific groups of people.

Unlike twenty years ago, hardly a day goes by that I don't encounter someone who tells me about their family member or friend who has autism. Through whatever means possible, help, such as appropriate living facilities, better access to healthcare, more research, respite care, better school programs, more training for medical personnel and police officers, and much more, for these children and adults must be put in place. To accomplish these goals, funding is always the major issue. The first priority should be raising awareness with our elected officials because starting there might result in increased allocations for the disabled.

About thirty years ago a friend of mine took her autistic son to our state capitol to speak to the legislature about autism. She said while they were waiting in the rotunda area, the echoes from the capitol dome made her son became very anxious, and he began yelling due to the overstimulation of the sounds in the building. She said a senator nearby noticed her son's behavior, and as he walked by he said to her, "If my child acted that way I would throw water in his face." Either that man had no clue about autism or was a very heartless person.

We need more elected officials like former Congressman Dan Burton of Indiana who is an autism advocate. He read my first book, and afterward

I received a very supportive letter in which he shared information about his grandson who has autism. In the letter he said, "We are in this battle together." Congressman Burton is a well-respected man, and his kind letter, as well as his advocacy for autism, demonstrates that it only takes one experience of having a family member diagnosed with autism to change a person's perspective on life and priorities.

Writing this book has not been an easy task because I am also caring daily for my vaccine-injured son and daughter. I'm not complaining; I'm simply illustrating that like so many other mothers and fathers in this situation, we are simply exhausted. We have little energy left over after meeting the daily requirements of caregiving. My days are filled with a multitude of tasks, such as giving medications, answering doctors' calls, making doctor appointments, going to appointments, traveling to the emergency room, refilling prescriptions, picking up prescriptions, filling out paperwork, buying groceries, cooking, and cleaning. In Stephen's case we have to shave him, help him dress, brush his teeth, bathe him, and more. Even so, I thank God that he has given me the strength to sit down and work on this book.

I tell people all the time that I don't want to sound like I'm complaining, and one of Stephen's doctors reminds me, "You're not complaining Mary, you're just reporting." I guess that's the best way of looking at it. The unique thing about autism is that it's not a one-time bump in the road; it's a lifelong journey. When Stephen's father and I are unable to care for him, something will need to already be in place to assure an appropriate living situation for Stephen, which is the concern of all parents like us. I frequently have parents ask me what's going to happen to their child. The answer is, I don't know. Our personal situation is a bit unique because we have no extended family members who can step in to care for Stephen. Laurel will never be able to assume the role as Stephen's caregiver due to her own health issues.

The good news is that Stephen is making progress in several areas that will hopefully contribute to a better quality of life for him in the future. For example, he is experiencing better seizure control, which in turn has greatly improved his behavior. The police are not being called in as often to help with him, which I hope will continue. Occasionally when we see one of our local officers out in public, they comment on how they haven't received calls from us in quite some time. One officer asked, "What have you done that has changed the need for us to come and help you with Stephen?" When I explained that we believe it's the new treatments and supplements we have been using that have really made such a difference in him, the officer said, "That's it?" I laughed and told her the only thing that has changed is fewer medications and more supplements, sunshine, Epsom salt baths, and a better diet. The officer just shook her head and said, "That's amazing." She was very happy to hear it is working for him.

Additionally, Stephen has a vagus nerve stimulator (VNS), implanted in his chest that helps control some seizure activity, and he is going to physical therapy once a week to help keep him active and strengthen his muscles. We continue to follow Dr. Seneff's recommended therapy of Epsom salt baths and sunshine and Dr. Blaylock's recommended supplements. We also carefully monitor Stephen's diet to make sure he eats healthy non-GMO foods.

Stephen is currently taking the following list of supplements on a rotating basis, based on a daily assessment of how he appears to be doing, because we don't want to overload his system. Some supplements are added to his smoothies.

1. D-ribose
2. MSM, an organic form of sulfur
3. Taurine
4. Tyrosine
5. Biotin (B7)
6. B6
7. B complex
8. Tart cherry juice
9. Probiotics

10. Baicalin

11. Coconut

12. Cayenne pepper capsules

13. Cal-mag-zinc

14. Magnesium citrate

15. Vitamin B12 sublingual spray

16. Advanced Glutathione sublingual spray.

17. D3

18. Omega 3

19. Methyl Folate – Stephen has MTHFR genetic mutation

20. Spirulina, a pre-biotic

21. Sufficient-C

Our most recent addition to Stephen's daily regimen is giving a daily dose of Charlotte's Web Premium Hemp Extract oil, which was recommended by his neurologist. Cannabidiol (CBD) is manufactured in Colorado by the Stanley Brothers and is legal in all fifty states. See the website, Realm of Caring. Stephen's neurologist said the Stanley Brothers offer a standardized form of CBD oil, which is important. The oil is reported to help with Lennox-Gastaut Syndrome, especially the serious drop seizures Stephen suffers.

Glutathione in a spray sublingual form has been added to Stephen's daily regimen based on information from Dr. Mark Hyman, M.D., who reports in an online blog that glutathione is, "The mother of all antioxidants." He says it's the most important molecule to stay healthy and prevent disease. Most importantly he states that glutathione is necessary to treat autism. Search online for "Essential Glutathione: Dr. Mark Hyman," and you can read the full article. We are also using Young Living essential oils with Stephen. Cayenne pepper has proven helpful for Stephen's constipation. As an infant, diarrhea was a huge problem, and then as he got older, constipation and a rectal fissure became an issue. Doctors prescribed lactulose for years to help with constipation and his high level of ammonia, but we have found that cayenne pepper capsules have worked better for him because it reportedly helps to stimulate the intestinal tract.

Efflux disorder is a condition associated with autism that I want to briefly address. In medical dictionaries it is defined as something that flows outward. Dr. H. Vasken Aposhian, PhD., is currently an emeritus professor of microbiology and cellular biology at the University of Arizona. He has published reports on efflux disorder, which he explains causes people with autism to have difficulty shedding toxins from their system. Dr. Aposhian has published more than 100 peer-reviewed studies on heavy metal poisoning. In 2004, Dr. Aposhian gave a slide presentation at an Institute of Medicine (IOM) meeting entitled, "A Toxicologists View of Thimerosal and Autism." In his slide presentation he questions whether autism is an efflux disorder. Dr. Aposhian states in one of his slides that, "It appears that autistic children lack an effective mercury efflux system." I have not been able to find a lot of information on the subject of efflux disorder and autism, but I believe that more research is needed on this topic. It may prove to be a significant piece of the autism puzzle.

In July 2016 we had an appointment scheduled for Stephen at Barnes-Jewish Hospital, in St. Louis, Missouri. We were planning to drive him for an evaluation there because the hospital is now performing a brain surgery called the amygdalohippocampectomy. The surgery can reportedly help with drop seizures in a high percentage of patients with LGS. However, before the surgery could be considered for Stephen, he would have needed an evaluation by a neurologist in St. Louis to determine if he might be a candidate. It is a relatively new surgery in the United States but has been performed in Europe for several years. We decided last minute not to make the long drive with Stephen for the evaluation because he most likely would not be a candidate, and we are not sure at this point if we actually would want to put him through such a serious brain surgery at his age. One of the down sides reported for that surgery is loss of memory, and I would not want that for Stephen.

The last thirty-five years have been filled with many days where we felt so desperate and hopeless about finding help for Stephen. Historically his behaviors have been head banging, breaking windows, knocking holes in walls, fighting, biting, throwing things, running away, and, of course, add having seizures to that list. I used to jokingly tell people that I would not recognize my house unless it had police cars, an ambulance, and fire trucks in the street in front of it. Humor is essential when you live a life like ours. There were times when the police had to be called as many as three times in one day to help us get Stephen under control during a meltdown. I know thousands of families are going down this same road, and I pray for them daily.

However, over the many years we have learned a lot from very informed people and found ways to improve Stephen's quality of life and remediate many of the issues that were causing Stephen so much seizure activity. My goal now is to ensure that someone will always be in his life to continue to implement what we have found to help Stephen, and most of all to tell him he is loved and valuable. As long as we are able, my husband and I will continue to provide for our children as well as prepare for their future needs.

Everyone in the autism community must continue to raise awareness and work toward creating a more compassionate world for all people with physical and mental challenges. I want to encourage and recognize that sometimes even the smallest display of kindness, such as Dr. Blaylock's ending comment in emails where he says, "May the Lord Bless you and Stephen," can leave a parent feeling encouraged that someone is supportive and understands.

I also want to recognize the tireless work that the Vaxxed team continues to do in raising awareness to put an end to vaccine injury, an important cause. On Vaxxed.com the site explains how Polly Tommey founded The Autism Trust charity in the United Kingdom in 2007, which has a facility in Berkshire. Recently in Austin, Texas, Polly formed a 501 (c) (3) non-profit foundation that plans to build an inspirational center offering both residential and outpatient resources to individuals living with autism. In 2010, Polly founded the Autism Media Channel that has produced over sixty videos for the European Sky Information Channel. Other ongoing key contributors for the Vaxxed movement are Dr. Andrew Wakefield, producer Del Bigtree, Polly's husband Jonathan, as well as her daughter Bella, son Billy, and son Toby. Billy was diagnosed with autism at the age of two years. For over a year, Polly and the Vaxxed team have been on the road traveling to different cities screening the movie *Vaxxed*, which is followed up with an audience question and answer session. A wonderful man named Anu is their current driver and videographer, and Dr. Suzanne Humphries has been traveling with them on the bus for several months.

The RV, in which they travel and do taped interviews, plays an integral part in their message. The outside of the RV is signed with the names of thousands of children who were vaccine injured. Inside the RV, there are photos that serve as a memorial and testimonial of the beautiful children and babies who tragically died after receiving vaccines. Polly and the team are gathering important information on the tours by listening to, and recording stories of both vaccine-injured children and those of healthy unvaccinated children and adults. They are technically doing their own vaccinated versus unvaccinated study. This is something that has never been done by pharmaceutical companies.

Robert Kennedy Jr., is also working on behalf of autistic children by meeting with lawmakers to raise awareness about the danger of thimerosal in vaccines, which is only one of many toxic adjuvants. Along with the Vaxxed team, he is also opposing new legislation in California that mandates vaccinations with no medical or religious exemptions. This requirement became effective July 1, 2016, through legislation signed by Governor Jerry Brown.

A growing number of informed caring doctors, researchers, therapists, parents, and caregivers are joining the battle to combat future vaccine damage to children and adults. Most have seen the movie *Vaxxed*, and they are now making every attempt to help get the message out to avoid future vaccine injuries. I believe a united effort to not vaccinate children will pay off in the long run and save many others from needless suffering.

On a personal note, I would like for all parents of vaccine-injured children to know that I will continue to pray for answers for you and your family. Always remember that you are your child's best advocate and voice. This book is not intended to recommend medications or procedures, supplements, diets, or essential oils for a child. Always check with a doctor before trying anything new. I hope my shared experiences and information are helpful on your autism journey.

INDEX

Asthma, 52, 61

Ataxia (loss of balance), 80

Atonic seizures (drop seizures), 31, 46, 67, 78, 89, 98, 120

Autism, 1, 10-11, 16, 18-19, 24-25, 30, 33-36, 39, 42-43, 55, 57, 60-62, 64-66, 74-75, 78-79, 84-86, 93-94, 99-102, 108, 117-118, 122

Autism: Maternally Derived Antibodies Specific for Fetal Brain Proteins, 83

Autism Research Institute (ARI), 28

Autism Society of America (ASA), 3, 28, 79

Autism Spectrum Disorders (ASD), 29, 48, 66, 81, 84-85

Autoimmune Reactions, 51-52, 61, 109

Autonomic Nervous System, 33, 52

B

B5, 81

B6, 28, 119

B7 (Biotin), 119

B12, 120

Bacteriophage (s), 103-108, 110-111, 113, 115-116

Baicalin, 97-98, 120

Barnes-Jewish Hospital, 121

B complex, 119

Bergman, Dr. John, D.C., 55, 73

Bigtree, Del, 60, 123

Biotin (B7), 119

Blaylock, Dr. Russell, M.D., 51-54, 96-99, 102, 109, 122

Borrelia Burgdorferi, 82

Choline, 99

Churchill Fellows' Silver Medallion Award, 106

Churchill, Sir Winston, 106

Clostridium Difficile (C-Diff), 103-104

Cobalamin, 99

Coconut, 120

Coconut oil, 97

Cognitive impairment, 101

Colorado State University, 27

Columbus, Christopher, 55

Community Based Waiver, 74, 77

Complex partial seizures, 32

Congenital transfer, 82

Constipation, 80, 120

Corn syrup, 99

Corpus Callosotomy (CC), 45

CPR, 20

Crisis Center, 40-41, 43

Crisis Intervention Team Officers, 66

Crohn's disease, 52

Cromolyn, 56

Cytokine (s), 52

D

D3 Sulfate, 101-102, 120

D3 Supplement, 101, 120

Delmont Laboratories, 104, 109-110, 115

Humoral immunity, 51

Humphries, Dr. Suzanne, M.D., 49, 53, 114-115, 123

Hyman, Dr. Mark, M.D., 120

I

Ictal, 32

Idiopathic seizures, 55

IGeneX, 81-82

Immune problems, 51, 55-56, 82-83, 100, 108, 116

Immunoexcitotoxicity, 52

Infantile Spasms, 13-14, 17, 30-31

Inflammation, 50, 53, 97

In-Home Community Based Waivered, 77

Institute of Medicine (IOM), 121

Intestinal disorders, 100

IP (Individual Plan), 75-77

Iron, 98-100

Ischemia (Impaired blood flow), 55

J

Judge Judy, 3

K

Kanner, Dr. Leo, M.D., 28

Kanner's Syndrome, 1, 2

Kennedy, Robert Jr., 123

Keppra, 56

Klinghardt, Dr. Dietrich, M.D., PhD., 83

MTHFR (Methylenetetrahydrofolate reductase), 120

Myoclonic seizures, 31-32, 35

N

National Childhood Vaccine Injury Act of 1986 (NCVIA), 50

National Vaccine Information Center (NVIC), 50

Nema, Howard, 116

NIH (National Institutes of Health), 14

Nitric oxide, 101

Non-floridated toothpaste, 100

Non-Hodgkin's Lymphoma, 54

Nutritionist, 75

Nystatin, 83

O

Occupational therapy (OT), 86

Olive oil, 97

Omega 3, 120

Oral Polio Vaccine, 50

P

Paravicini, Derek, 26

Peek, Kim, 26-27

Perlmutter, Dr. David, M.D., 57

Perseveration, 3

Pertussis, 2, 12, 50

Petit Mal seizures, 32

Phage (s), 106, 108-109, 111- 113, 116

Texas, Lubbock, 106, 112

Th1, 51

Th2, 51

Thiamine, 101

Thimerosal, 12, 48, 123

Thomas, John P., 54

Thompson, Dr. William, PhD., 60

Tobey, Charles Jr., 115-116

Tobey, Gov. Charles William Sr., 115

Tommey, Polly, 58, 60, 63-64, 122-123

Tommey, Jonathan, Bella, Billy, Toby, 123

Tonic clonic, 31

Tribeca Film Festival, 61

Truth Talk News, 116

Twort, Dr. Fredrick William, FRS., 110

Tylenol, 13

Tyrosine, 119

U
UC Davis 2007 Study, 83

UK (United Kingdom), 109

V
Vaccine (s), 10, 12, 48 56, 58, 60-61, 83, 103, 107, 123

Vaccine Injury Compensation Program (VICP), 50

Vagus Nerve Stimulator (VNS), 119

Vaidya, Anu, 123

VAXXED, 60-61, 122-123

W

Waivered Services, 75-77, 86

Wakefield, Dr. Andrew, MB, BS, FRCS, FRCPath, Academic Gastroenterologist, 58, 60, 63-64, 116, 123

Wenner, Melinda, 108

West Syndrome, 13, 30-31

Wetmore, Koren, 112

Williams, Kathi, 50

Wiltshire, Stephen, 27

Winston Churchill Memorial Trust, 105

Winston Churchill Traveling Fellowship, 105

Women In War, 107

X

Xanax, 56

Y

Yeast overgrowth, 101

YouTube, 26, 39, 49, 51-52, 55, 82, 99, 106-107, 111

Z

Zinc, 99- 101